Teachers Who Learn Kids Who Achieve

A Look at Schools with Model Professional Development

WestEd

WestEd is a research, development, and service agency working with education and other communities to promote excellence, achieve equity, and improve learning for children, youth, and adults. Drawing on the best knowledge from research and practice, we work with practitioners, policymakers, and others to address education's most critical issues. A nonprofit agency, WestEd, whose work extends internationally, serves as one of the nation's designated regional educational laboratories — originally created by Congress in 1966 — serving the states of Arizona, California, Nevada, and Utah. With headquarters in San Francisco, WestEd has offices across the United States.

For more information about WestEd, visit our Web site, call, or write:

WestEd®
730 Harrison Street
San Francisco, CA 94107-1242
415/565-3000
877/4WestEd (toll-free)
www.WestEd.org

This document was produced in whole or in part with funds from the Office of Educational Research and Improvement, U.S. Department of Education, under contract number RJ96006901. Its contents do not necessarily reflect the views or policies of the Department of Education.

Contents

Tables and Sidebars

Acknowledgments

The National Awards Program for Model Professional Development does more than acknowledge and celebrate exemplary efforts. It also provides a resource from which others can learn. As part of an effort to make the insights from these successful schools available to others, the U.S. Department of Education asked WestEd to examine the eight schools that won the award in the first two years of the competition, 1996-97 and 1997-98, and to tease out the factors leading to their success. (Several districts were also recognized, but their stories are beyond the scope of this study.)

To undertake this study on a rapid timeline, WestEd was fortunate to be able to subcontract with Joellen Killion and the National Staff Development Council. The long-term work of both Killion and the organization equipped them to learn quickly and to appreciate the extraordinary features of these schools. Working with a team of researchers from the two organizations, Killion orchestrated site visits, case reports, and cross-site analysis. The initial research report (accessible on WestEd's Web site: www.WestEd.org/WestEd/news.html/) provides the details of her thorough analysis of trends across the eight sites. The team of researchers included Ann Abeille, Vivian Elliott, Nancy Hurley, Treseen McCormick, Cindy McPherson, Renya Ramirez, Dolores Sandoval, and Susan Schiff.

Distilling the information from the research into the present document was the task of a set of writers and editors at WestEd. Thanks are due to the primary writers Jim Johnson and Lynn Murphy. Design assistance was provided by Max McConkey and the staff of Visual Strategies. The cover photos are the work of Nita Winter.

The identification of these schools as award winners would not have been possible without the continuing efforts of staff from the Regional Educational Laboratories who have worked with the U.S. Department of Education over the past several years to design and conduct the awards program. Laboratory staff also provided valuable input to this document.

The report that follows is based on hundreds of hours talking with teachers and administrators at these eight schools. We appreciate their graciousness in welcoming visitors into their schools in the closing weeks of the school year and their openness in sharing the stories behind their success.

Nikola N. Filby
Coordinator of the Regional Laboratory Program
WestEd
February 2000

Introduction

When a low-performing school turns around, what can we learn? In a district where one school has twice the achievement gains of comparable schools, what is going on? If a school is able to eliminate performance gaps between its white and non-white students, shouldn't we pay attention?

The eight schools represented in this report tell the story of students who achieve because their teachers are learners. Whether the school is in a rural community of Texas *colonias* or a privileged Georgia suburb, whether students have a transiency rate of 126 percent or a poverty rate of 88 percent, the culture of learning is palpable. Teachers, paraprofessionals, and administrators have coalesced as learning communities and focused their own learning on what will translate into learning for students. Everyone is learning, and everyone benefits.

At the heart of each school's success is an exemplary professional development program — one we can profitably examine. How, exactly, did the staffs in these schools choose and maintain a focus, organize their time, and create a collaborative environment? And how did their professional development efforts interact with some of the conditions we already know are basic to successful school reform?

In this report you will find specifics, exactly which literacy program a Colorado school chose five years ago, for example. But our

Principles of Effective Professional Development

The mission of professional development is to prepare and support educators to help all students achieve to high standards of learning and development. When professional development is effective, a number of principles can be identified. In particular, it

- Focuses on teachers as central to student learning, yet includes all other members of the school community;
- Focuses on individual, collegial, and organizational improvement;
- Respects and nurtures the intellectual and leadership capacity of teachers, principals, and others in the school community;
- Reflects best available research and practice in teaching, learning, and leadership;
- Enables teachers to develop further expertise in subject content, teaching strategies, uses of technologies, and other essential elements in teaching to high standards;
- Promotes continuous inquiry and improvement embedded in the daily life of schools;
- Is planned collaboratively by those who will participate in and facilitate that development;
- Requires substantial time and other resources;
- Is driven by a coherent long-term plan;
- Is evaluated ultimately on the basis of its impact on teacher effectiveness and student learning; and this assessment guides subsequent professional development efforts.

focus is on more general conclusions, such as why that instructional program, or another one built around Navajo culture, or another one about math problem solving, or one about thinking skills have all been successful for anchoring professional development. We will help you analyze the role of programs like these in successful professional development. Likewise, if you want specific information about the implementation approaches in these schools — from Title I-funded coaching through voluntary Saturdays, it's here. But so too is an analysis of why a whole range of implementation strategies can work.

Finally, if you want to know what any of these analyses mean specifically for you, in your role as a principal, teacher, or district administrator, we have also organized our findings with your needs in mind. Our goal, after all, is to help you think about how *you* might apply the learnings from these schools to the professional development efforts you already have under way or are about to get started. What the schools in this report have accomplished is worthy of our attention not just because they have been successful, but because their models can help others to be so as well.

The awards program is based on a set of principles of effective professional development. They are enumerated on the facing page. (More information about the awards program itself can be found on page 4.)

These schools are worthy of our attention not just because they have been successful, but because their models can help others to be so as well.

National Awards Program for Model Professional Development

The National Awards Program for Model Professional Development honors schools (and districts) for their comprehensive efforts to increase teacher and student learning through professional development. But the awards program has another purpose as well. It promotes these successful efforts as models that others can learn from. As Secretary of Education Richard Riley explained in launching the program, "We need to do more to professionalize teaching. As we ask more and more of today's teachers, we must provide the necessary support to enable them to teach to high standards. High quality professional development is one critical component to meet this challenge."

HOW TO APPLY

When you think about what your own school has been able to accomplish for students, is there a story of successful professional development to tell? Are there clear relationships between teacher learning and measurable achievement for *all* students? Can you point to particular things that helped to shift the culture in your school to one that is relentless about learning – for students and for staff? Will other schools be able to apply your experience to their own?

To be considered for national recognition, applicants should be able to demonstrate that their program of professional development is a comprehensive model, for any grades from pre-K through 12, that exemplifies the Department of Education's Mission and Principles of Professional Development. In other words, award-winning programs will have professional growth as an integral part of school culture, address the needs of all students served, and promote professional development practices that ensure equity by being free of bias and accessible to all educators. Recognition under the awards program is based on how well applicants demonstrate that their professional development programs result in increased student learning.

Award applications and information about award winners are available online. Check the U.S. Department of Education's Web site for teachers:

www.ed.gov/inits/teachers/96-97/

www.ed.gov/inits/teachers/97-98/

The Eight Schools

While similar in their achievements, these eight award-winning schools represent a wide range of locations, sizes, and student characteristics. Whatever your particular school setting, aspects of one or more of these schools are likely to sound familiar. Perhaps the most salient thing suggested by these winners of the National Awards Program for Model Professional Development is that school demographics need not foreclose school success.

At the surface level, these exemplary schools are diverse. They are scattered across the country, from Roxbury, Massachusetts, to Manhattan, Kansas, to El Paso, Texas. Students range from kindergarten age to 21-year-olds. In some schools the vast majority of students are Latino; in others they are white, or African American, or Navajo. In one school fewer than 3 percent of the students receive free or reduced-price lunch, while in some others the percentage is over 80. The largest school runs year-round and has 860 students; the smallest schools serve fewer than 300 children.

As award recipients, however, these schools do share one easily discernable characteristic: their students have all made important academic gains. Teacher learning has paid off in measurable success for students. The table on page 8, "Overview of Eight Award-Winning Schools," provides a quick look at the most basic information about these schools, as well as at the ways each has measured success.

Below, each school is also introduced with a few broad strokes — snapshots to differentiate one school from another. (In Appendix A, profiles of the eight schools introduce each school and its distinctive professional development effort in more detail.)

Ganado Intermediate School is on a Navajo reservation in Ganado, Arizona. Most students are English language learners and receive free or reduced-price lunch. A professional development focus on literacy and Navajo language and culture has raised student test scores and, at the same time, narrowed the male-female achievement gap. Another success has been an increase in the number of Navajo teachers.

H.D. Hilley Elementary School sits just across the Texas border from Mexico, and the vast majority of its students are poor and Latino. Demographics might predict low student achievement, but at Hilley, impressive gains in state assessment scores led to the school's recognition as a 1997 Texas Successful School.

Hungerford School, P.S. 721R in Staten Island, serves a special education population of 12- to 21-year-olds. In focusing on how to increase students' independent functioning, Hungerford staff have been able to increase students' inclusion in general education classes, the achievement of goals in students' Individual Education Plans (IEPs), and the number of students placed in jobs.

International High School at LaGuardia Community College serves a student population made up of immigrants and English language learners. Students speak 37 different languages, but the staff has been able to narrow the achievement gap for students whose home language is not English, as well as increase students' attendance, graduation, and college acceptance rates.

Mason Elementary School, with an urban student population that is 71 percent African American, doubled its enrollment over a five-year period, moving from the 79th most-chosen to the 12th most-chosen school in its Boston district. Standardized test gains were almost double those districtwide after the first three years of a focused professional development effort.

Montview Elementary School has close to 900 students and a transciency rate of 126 percent. Professional development embedded in a schoolwide literacy program helped the staff take students' reading and math scores from below the district average to the top of the district range, while virtually eliminating the performance gap between white and non-white students.

Shallowford Falls Elementary School is a suburban school with almost no English language learners and almost no students receiving free or reduced-price lunch. Ninety percent of its students are white. With no demographic challenges, but dissatisfied with students' achievement, the staff plunged into the Georgia Pay for Performance program, becoming one of only ten schools in the state to receive a merit pay grant in 1994 and winning a second grant in 1998.

Woodrow Wilson Elementary School shares a pleasant college town with Kansas State University and has made the most of that proximity. When a new state math assessment left Wilson students in the dust, the staff involved the university and looked to professional development to turn things around. Starting out with a focus on math problem solving, and then adding literacy, they were able to increase student performance across the board.

Overview of Eight Award-Winning Schools

School	Grades	Number of Students	Student Ethnicity
Ganado Intermediate School *Ganado, Arizona*	3–5	515	99% Navajo
H.D. Hilley Elementary School *El Paso, Texas*	K–5	690	89% Latino 11% White 1% African American
Hungerford School, P.S. 721R *Staten Island, New York*	12 to 21 years old	250	59% White 20% African American 15% Latino 6% Asian
International High School at LaGuardia Community College *Long Island City, New York*	9–12	450	45% Latino 30% Asian 22% White 2% African American
Samuel W. Mason Elementary School *Roxbury, Massachusetts*	K–5	300	71% African American 14% White 11% Latino 2% Asian 2% Native American
Montview Elementary School *Aurora, Colorado*	K–5	860	46% Latino 27% African American 21% White 5% Asian 1% Native American
Shallowford Falls Elementary School *Marietta, Georgia*	K–5	660	90% White 3% African American 3% Latino 3% Asian
Woodrow Wilson Elementary School *Manhattan, Kansas*	K–6	320	80% White 15% African American 3% Asian 1% Latino 1% Native American

English Language Learners	***Free/Reduced Lunch***	***Special Needs***	***Measures of Success***
68%	88%	11%	• increased norm-referenced test scores • narrowed gender achievement gap • narrowed ELL achievement gap • increased number of Navajo teachers • increased parent participation
24%	70%	9%	• 1997 Texas Successful School • increased state assessment scores
14%	67%	100%	• more students use technology • increased job placements • more students achieve IEPs • more students included in general education
73%* ** 100% when admitted*	82%	0%	• increased graduation rates • increased attendance rates • increased college acceptance rates • narrowed ELL achievement gap
23%*	74%	26%	• doubled enrollment • went from 79th most-chosen to 12th most-chosen school in district • almost doubled districtwide test scores gains
42%	77%	13% 126% * **student transiency*	• increased reading and math scores from below district average to district high • virtually eliminated ethnicity performance gaps • selected as Literacy Learning Network demonstration site
0.5%	3%	15%	• steadily higher ITBS scores even with baseline scores above district average • selected as Talents Unlimited demonstration site
1%	44%	30%	• increased student performance in math • increased student performance in science • increased student performance in reading and language arts

The Key: A Culture of Learning

This whole process of staff development must be part of the culture and not something peripheral. That's why it's so effective.

— Teacher, Montview Elementary School

Teacher learning made a difference at these eight schools because it was part of a change in professional culture. The very nature of staff development shifted from isolated learning and the occasional workshop to focused, ongoing organizational learning built on collaborative reflection and joint action. This was the key finding from an extensive study of the eight schools.

The central importance of a professional community — a culture of learning — will be no surprise to those familiar with other educational research. It is increasingly clear that the skill-training model of professional development is not enough, even when the training is followed up with guided practice and coaching, long emphasized as neglected pieces of that model. Substantial progress is made only when teacher learning becomes embedded in the school day and the regular life of the school. (A list of resources on page 48 identifies some of the major writings in this area.)

The value of this study is not only to provide further evidence that a culture of learning is crucial, but also to provide concrete examples of what it means: What distinguishes a professional learning community? What does it look like? How did these eight schools get there?

As described in Appendix B, site teams visited each of the schools, interviewed teachers and administrators, and then described what they learned on in a number of ways. The study was guided by two broad questions:

- What teacher learning opportunities are available in these schools?
- How do teachers learn?

These questions led to others, as site visitors sought to understand how each school had made progress, from the perspectives not only of reform leaders but of "every teacher." Six broad lessons emerged, exemplified across the eight schools. They are listed in the box below and each is elaborated in the chapter sections that follow: "Student-Centered Goals," "An Expanded Definition of Professional Development," "Ongoing, Job-Embedded Informal Learning," "A Collaborative Environment," "Time for Learning and Collaboration," and "Checking for Results."

Lessons Learned

- Use clear, agreed-upon student achievement goals to focus and shape teacher learning.
- Provide an expanded array of professional development opportunities.
- Embed ongoing, informal learning into the school culture.
- Build a highly collaborative school environment where working together to solve problems and to learn from each other become cultural norms.
- Find and use the time to allow teacher learning to happen.
- Keep checking a broad range of student performance data.

STUDENT-CENTERED GOALS

> *Schoolwide professional development is aligned and embedded in the school improvement plan. Grade-level and individual professional development is also aligned with school goals and student needs. The latest fad or entertaining speaker has no place in the school.*
>
> — Teacher, Shallowford Falls Elementary School

Clear, student-centered goals have focused teacher learning in each of these schools. Each in its different way identified and translated important student needs into a plan for action, creating shared goals for raising achievement in every classroom and across grades. Such a plan becomes the driver and the yardstick for teacher growth. It channels learning, energy, and commitment; serves to screen and shape professional development activities; and becomes the gauge for teachers' progress and success.

Looking at this goal-building process across the eight schools, at how staff reached consensus around concrete, student-centered school improvement aims and chose instructional programs to foster them, several common points stand out.

First, these goals don't spring into being overnight. They grow out of an intensive, collaborative process of looking hard at where the school is now and how students are performing across the curriculum, and then deciding where the school wants to go. At each school visited, a student-focused planning process, usually linked to formal requirements, was in place before dramatic change became visible. At Woodrow Wilson, the Kansas Quality Performance Accreditation program requires an annual plan for improvement with specific student achievement goals. Similarly, at H.D. Hilley, the Texas Campus Improvement Plan establishes the expectations for continuous

Evolving Goals at Shallowford Falls Elementary

In 1990, when Shallowford Falls Elementary School was about to open its doors for the first time, the staff's single most important goal was to learn each other's names. Eight years later, when the school was recognized for having one of the most effective staff development programs in the country, staff members had learned a lot more than how to greet each other. But in that first overnight staff retreat, which has become a school tradition, they started with names and team building. They had to.

The focus for professional development in those first years came from the administration and reflected what the principal had told teachers when she hired them: "We will work as a team." Because this statement had relevance for school governance, not just staff attitudes, early professional development also took teachers through training in site-based management and decisionmaking.

Once Georgia instituted its Pay for Performance program, the principal asked teachers to consider taking part in it. That program's model of carefully documenting gains in student learning was one that resonated at Shallowford Falls. Aligning professional development with a fine-grained analysis of students' standardized test scores, within the framework of county goals and state standards, has become one of the school hallmarks.

Each year, the Building Leadership Team, which has representatives from each grade level, special education, specialist teachers, paraprofessionals, and other support staff, develops the School Improvement Plan. This team collects student data, talks with people whom they represent, and drafts a School Improvement Plan for consideration by the entire staff. Before the plan is voted on, everyone has seen it and given input several times. It is everyone's plan and everyone's responsibility.

One year, for example, they voted to embark on a three-year effort that would take the whole staff through the Frameworks literacy program – working in heterogeneous groups. "It was interesting for people to see how reading evolved across the grades and how to provide kids with consistency and continuity," one teacher recalls.

Literacy has continued to be a focus in subsequent years, along with Talents Unlimited, a program to improve students' critical and creative thinking skills in content areas. More recently, technology has become an additional focus, again linked to student learning goals.

A teacher who was a charter member of the Shallowford Falls faculty sums up how the school's professional development goals have changed over the years: "Our first school goals dealt with bonding and being a team. Nothing was very specific or academic. But we've evolved into very specific academic goals. Each year we grow in our ability to set goals."

These goals don't spring into being overnight.

growth. Hungerford's curriculum committees set standards for student performance that align with its district improvement plan. The Coordinating Council at International High School determines the focus of all faculty-run committees based on extensive teacher input. Everyone in these successful schools knows the goals and supports them. Then, with a clear sense of what results they want, all work together to achieve them.

Often the process started small, focusing initially on one or two specific areas, and then, with growing success, expanding to others. Teachers at Woodrow Wilson initially set out to improve their students' mathematical problem solving and ended by raising student performance not only in math but in science and writing, as well. Quite often, in fact, these award-winning schools focused early reform efforts on issues not at the heart of classroom practice — such as increasing parent involvement or improving staff relationships — only gradually shifting more directly to issues of teaching and learning. International High School staff point out that starting "small" was critical to their success. Smaller, they believe, means more control and flexibility, and rapid response to issues that arise. Begin with just one change, they suggest, perhaps starting with a teacher portfolio process, and then bring that to the student level. But do it thoroughly and deeply.

Using test results and student data to identify specific areas for improvement, these schools selected or designed interventions to help tackle them. Montview saw the need for more consistency in reading instruction across grade levels, and after a few teachers piloted a Literacy Learning Network program with remarkable success, the entire staff decided to implement it schoolwide.

"The principal asked us, 'What do you want for the students? What is your wish list?' Boy, did we brainstorm."

At Ganado Intermediate, student-centered goals were developed from the staff's vision of what they wanted for their students. As one teacher recalls:

> *A couple of months into the school year the principal asked us, 'What do you want for the students? What is your wish list?' Boy, did we brainstorm. We talked about what we hoped for and wanted down to the grade level. She had us project five years from the time we brainstormed. That's how we started.*

Focusing on language and literacy to raise student achievement, Ganado's five-year professional development plan included English as a Second Language, writing, Navajo culture and language, Collaborative Literature Intervention Program (CLIP), and technology.

In every case such choices are guided by student improvement goals. "There needs to be a vision," one teacher at Samuel Mason school explains:

> *And there needs to be a process for how you're going to achieve it. Once you can get through those things — and they are painful, working as unified as you possibly can with the understanding that sometimes you just have to live with it because it is what's best for the population at large — you develop an understanding of what everyone's doing and where we're going. And through this process we always go back and ask if this is what we want: Does it match the vision? Is it what we want for our children? And if you can answer yes to both of them, then you know it's something to look into.*

The process takes time. As student and teacher needs are continually assessed, as new ideas are tried out, the plans themselves may change. A good example of this incremental forward motion is the

What teachers learn is driven by student needs.

path of change at Shallowford Falls. The principal describes how the beginning year's goals were weak, focusing on such things as bonding as a staff and physical aspects of the school plant. The second and third years' goals targeted improving working relationships and self-esteem. Then the Georgia Department of Education offered an opportunity to apply for merit pay. Through this Pay for Performance program volunteer schools were required to identify rigorous goals tied to improving students' academic performance. Shallowford Falls teachers, now comfortable enough as a staff to challenge themselves with more significant goals, focused on literacy and, eventually, expanded that focus to include the entire instructional program. (For more details, see page 14, "Evolving Goals at Shallowford Elementary.")

In each of these professional development programs, what teachers learn is driven by student needs — across the whole school, at specific grade levels, and in individual classrooms. This sustained focus over time is also key to ensuring the follow-through and reinforcement that make professional learning pay off, and it provides an axial point around which an increasingly collaborative learning culture develops. The point to emphasize here is that in each of these schools, the improvement plan drives teacher learning. It's both compass and touchstone, preventing professional development from being peripheral, disconnected, or fragmentary, and making it serve established needs for instructional improvement. An H.D. Hilley teacher sums it up this way: "Before, it felt like everyone was doing his or her own thing. Now it feels like the whole school is pulling together, trying to meet the goals that we have all discussed and created together. It feels like learning is seeping out of the school walls!"

Professional Development Planning Tools

Several guidebooks and toolkits offer schools practical tips for working through the professional development planning process.

NORTH CENTRAL REGIONAL EDUCATIONAL LABORATORY

Professional Development, Learning from the Best: A Toolkit for Schools and Districts Based on Model Professional Development Award Winners. Preview, download, or order a print copy of this 102-page resource. Includes sections on designing, implementing, and evaluating professional development.

www.ncrel.org/pd/

WESTED

Comprehensive School Reform: Research-Based Strategies to Achieve High Standards. This package includes two videotapes and a guidebook. The guidebook provides a coherent framework for planning schoolwide improvements aimed at helping every student meet challenging standards. The first videotape overviews the CSRD program; the other showcases several schools that have begun implementing schoolwide reform. The package is available for $59.

www.WestEd.org/

NORTHWEST REGIONAL EDUCATIONAL LABORATORY

A key part of planning is having a real understanding of students and their needs. The School Change Collaborative of the Regional Educational Laboratories, in their project on Students as Partners in Self Study, is field testing a variety of tools to capture student perspectives.

www.nwrel.org/scpd/natspec/dataday.html/

SERVE

Achieving Your Vision of Professional Development: How to Assess Your Needs and Get What You Want: This in-depth guide has sections on developing a vision, planning, and investing in professional development, with many examples. A chapter on the national award-winning schools is also included.

www.serve.org/publications/improve.htm/

AN EXPANDED DEFINITION OF PROFESSIONAL DEVELOPMENT

> *In our movement toward becoming a community of learners, P.S. 721 R encouraged all staff and parents to become "students" in the course of the daily activities of our school. As such, professional development is not separate from student instruction. It is an extension of learning throughout the school. Success for all students depends upon both the learning of the individual school employees and improvement of the capacity of the school to solve problems and renew itself.*
>
> — TEACHER, HUNGERFORD SCHOOL (P.S. 721 R)

Building the knowledge and skill necessary to carry out a school's improvement goals requires an array of professional development experiences. Teachers in all eight schools learn in a variety of ways, both formally and informally, from outside experts, building trainers, and from each other. All forms are necessary for continuous growth.

Formal learning is often the place schools start, in order to focus on specific content or to benefit from a well-established learning structure. But in our interviews, teachers repeatedly stressed that while formal training sets the stage, it's really through more informal modes that new ideas take root, spread, and become part of daily practice, and that the crucial habits of collegial sharing become ingrained.

As part of their improvement plans, all these schools have tapped outside expertise through traditional learning opportunities — workshops, district or school inservices, coursework, training sessions, and conferences. These usually involve a defined learning group, such as a team, department, or grade level, and have predetermined outcomes and prescribed learning processes, each designed and facilitated by an expert.

When school staff engage in training together, they come away with a shared set of ideas to try out and a common understanding of problems to grapple with as a team.

A four-day introduction to Literacy Learning Network, for example, gave Montview Elementary teachers the early tools they needed to begin whole-school implementation. As part of their plan to improve student literacy, teachers at Ganado Intermediate attended Northern Arizona Writing Project summer institutes. Samuel W. Mason teachers got extensive training in using Math Investigations and Early Literacy Learning Initiative (ELLI). Teachers at Woodrow Wilson attended workshops to gain more instructional strategies to teach problem solving in mathematics. Several schools had inservice technology courses. Teachers most appreciated on-site training designed to meet the specific needs of their school. These workshops were presented by outside consultants, district experts, and, occasionally, the school's teachers or principal.

Formal learning opportunities like these can strengthen teachers' content knowledge, introduce them to new instructional approaches, and explain the theories or principles underlying them. Moreover, these regularly scheduled sessions can also help get things moving. When school staff engage in training together, they come away with a shared set of ideas to try out and a common understanding of problems to grapple with as a team — and they discover all the while a natural focus for beginning a collaboration. Yet as comprehensive change efforts teach us, it's not enough to be exposed to new ideas, we have to know where they fit, and we have to become skilled in using them. These formal professional development structures can't ensure that the new knowledge will translate into strong classroom practice, that the skills will be honed in ways that lead to achievement of schoolwide goals.

The Knowledge Loom
Where Educators Craft Best Practice into Real World Success

"Professional development should be primarily school-based and built into the day-to-day work of teaching.

Teachers learn from their work. Learning how to teach more effectively on the basis of experience requires that such learning be planned for and evaluated. Learning needs arise and should be met in real contexts. Curriculum development, assessment, and decision-making processes are all occasions for learning. When built into these routine practices, professional development powerfully addresses real needs."

This is one of eight characteristics of effective professional development identified in the Web-based resource called "The Knowledge Loom," developed by the LAB at Brown University. The Web site includes a growing collection of varied best-practices resources. Those focused on professional development are consistent with the lessons in this report. The initial collection of school stories are from these award-winning schools. More vignettes will be added over time. Check this Web site for more good ideas, or to add your own.

http://knowledgeloom.org/

Joellen Killion compares formal training to the first steps in constructing a house: gathering the materials, blueprints, and tools needed to build it. But assembling the plan, equipment, and supplies is only part of the construction process. Actually building the house requires applying these tools and materials in highly collaborative ways, working together to produce results that match the plan. But here, adapting the analogy to school improvement, it's a question of building on what you know, learning new techniques for house framing and roofing as you go. In other words, informal approaches expand professional development to include, as Michael Fullan says, "learning while doing and learning from doing."

ONGOING, JOB-EMBEDDED INFORMAL LEARNING

> *Staff development is much, much more than 20 hours of required experiences. In fact, most of the staff development occurs informally, through asking for assistance from colleagues, sharing ideas, team meetings, attending conferences, or hearing what people learned from a particular speaker. The fourth Thursday of every month is always a staff development faculty meeting and those sessions usually incorporate new information and knowledge, practicing a skill or dialoguing within the team, or reviewing content learned previously.*
>
> — TEACHER, SHALLOWFORD FALLS

What teachers told us, repeatedly, is that the everyday work of schooling is, itself, an occasion for learning. Because teacher learning is so ingrained in their schools' culture, any opportunity for conversation can spontaneously turn into an occasion for learning. As one International High School teacher says, "Every conversation between two professionals is professional development. I think it's one of the main reasons this school has enjoyed so much success."

But this kind of professional culture developed only over time through the deliberate cultivation of collaborative structures at the school. Teachers participated in team meetings, grade-level meetings, and interdisciplinary curriculum development groups. They were part of study groups, action research groups, and dialogue sessions. In fact, the sheer number of different arrangements for teacher collaboration and conversation about teaching and learning was striking (see "Informal Learning Structures," page 23).

Some informal learning structures — important examples being peer and expert coaching — have traditionally been considered

Informal Learning Structures Identified by Teachers

- Analyzing student performance
- Attending content-area meetings
- Being observed by other teachers
- Coaching
- Conducting action research
- Conducting trial-and-error experiments
- Conversing with colleagues
- Creating student learning activities
- Creating teacher portfolios
- Designing curriculum
- Implementing new ideas
- Interacting with visiting professors
- Making decisions
- Mentoring
- Observing other teachers
- Observing students
- Organizing educational initiatives
- Participating in meetings
- Participating in self-studies
- Planning the budget
- Planning with grade-level team
- Reading articles and books
- Serving as a peer evaluator
- Serving on committees
- Serving on a leadership team
- Sharing from conferences
- Solving problems
- Studying student work
- Supervising a student teacher, intern, or teaching assistant
- Traveling
- Visiting other schools
- Watching videotapes
- Working on classroom, school, district, or community projects
- Working through conflicts
- Writing action plans
- Writing for professional publications
- Writing grants

follow-up. Occurring after a formal training experience, they help teachers take what they've learned so far and make it work in the classroom. Coaching, whether by fellow staff or outside consultants, helps teachers to reexamine what they have been taught, figure out how to integrate it into their current instructional and curricular

Coaching at Montview Elementary School*

Reviewing her schedule for Thursday, Renata sees that Julia, her teacher leader, will come in as usual for a weekly observation during her reading lesson. She reminds herself to review her action plan before their meeting and to make sure that Carol, the paraprofessional, has been scheduled to cover her classroom while she meets with Julia after the observation.

Renata remembers that initially she was concerned and very self-conscious about the coaching process; constructive feedback was sometimes hard for her to take. Working with Julia, though, Renata has found that while Julia is, herself, knowledgeable about reading, she lets Renata know that it's okay not to have all the answers, that, in fact, it's important to be able to ask questions.

When they meet to talk about a lesson, they focus on Renata's action plan – the one she made for herself – and talk about how it played out in the lesson. One thing they don't talk about is how to "fix" the lesson. Referring to specific things she observes, Julia often asks, "Why do you think that happened?" Sometimes they agree, sometimes they don't. But if they don't, they explore further, and that's when it's really the most fun.

Over the last few weeks, Renata has based her action plans on the kinds of questions she asks during reading group. The students, she felt, had not been taking responsibility for their learning. So during the lessons, Julia wrote down the questions Renata asked. As soon as she and Julia looked at the questions together, Renata realized she was doing way too much prompting. She was taking so much responsibility for the students' success that they didn't have to. Julia and Renata talked about what the questions would be like if she were to gradually release responsibility to the kids. Renata's questions during subsequent lessons started to change.

Julia also recommended some articles about questioning strategies that she and Renata could read and discuss. In fact, Renata had built one of those new strategies into the lesson Julia would see on Thursday....

* This vignette is constructed from the experiences of several Montview teachers.

unit, and gauge its effectiveness. In these schools, coaches often include peers, who are able to observe and help each other on a routine basis. Teachers see themselves participating in processes that allow one professional to help another learn and grow. (See page 24, "Coaching at Montview Elementary School.")

At these schools, informal learning has an additional significance. Because the thinking is not outside-in, informal structures like coaching are not seen as only one part of a more "comprehensive" training; instead, training is considered to be only one part of an ongoing process of teacher learning.

At the heart of informal learning is inquiry. These teachers want to understand their students and how they learn.

With this mindset in place, teachers can create opportunities for sharing and learning within their daily work. In the hall or lunchroom one teacher might mention to another, "I'm having trouble getting three of my students to finish editing their final writing project. You've gotten all your kids to finish. What strategies did you use?" Teachers talk over lunch about individual students, trade ideas about assessments in grade-level meetings, and discuss curriculum integration in cross-disciplinary teams. They serve on leadership teams, plan units of instruction, and share what works with each other. The power of this kind of learning is that it's practical and immediately relevant to what teachers do in their classrooms.

At the heart of many of these structures and processes is inquiry: disciplined study of what works in the local context. These teachers want to understand their students and how they learn. They ask questions and reflect on what is or isn't happening. They look to theory, research, and each other for promising practices to try out. They examine student work closely to analyze student learning and get clues for improvement. They try things out and study the effects over time. Again, these inquiry processes have become embedded in how these schools operate. But the schools have also used some explicit structures such as teacher study groups or teacher research projects. (See page 27, "Action Research at Wilson Elementary School," for the story of how one school staff incorporated action research to investigate and improve their practices in mathematics instruction.)

A COLLABORATIVE ENVIRONMENT

> *If there are four of you moving a piano up a staircase, you're going to work together, because you're jointly responsible for that piano. But if you were each taking a box of books upstairs, you wouldn't have to work together. So the principal has set up a school, and though there were a lot of other people involved, in some fundamental way he has made it possible for us to have a school where we're lugging a piano up the stairs together. We're so interdependent — it's in our best interest to work together.*
>
> — TEACHER, INTERNATIONAL HIGH SCHOOL

The kind of powerful collaborative learning these teachers describe doesn't just happen. In fact, traditional school organization works against it, walling teachers off from one another. "Almost everything about school," Linda Darling-Hammond and Milbrey McLaughlin observe, "is oriented toward going it alone professionally. Few schools are structured to allow teachers to think in terms of shared problems and broader organizational goals." All eight of these schools found ways to reverse this model, to break down the walls. Through explicit expectations and deliberate structuring, each built over time a supportive community of practice.

Action Research at Wilson Elementary School*

"We started an action-research project in 1995," explains Francie, a lead math teacher. "We had been getting math scores from the state since 1993, and Woodrow Wilson's scores were the lowest in the district. It was really embarrassing. When three of us signed up for an action-research class at Kansas State University, we saw it as an opportunity to deal with our students' problem-solving skills. We thought that if all our teachers, grades K-6, were knowledgeable about what students are expected to know on the assessment [which is given in grade 4] and were trained in the techniques for teaching and assessing open-ended math problems, the students would score higher over time.

"So we presented our proposal to the faculty. Not everyone was 100 percent behind the project, but they participated. First we got together and, looking at the state math assessment scores, we asked one another, 'What are we missing here?'"

Kit, who teaches fourth grade, reports what a revelation it was simply to take a hard look at the test. "We almost cried when we saw the exam. We were used to basic math, mostly a numbers test. We were comfortable with that type of test because that's what we were used to teaching. The new test had lots of reading and no two problems were alike. They had big blank areas, and now you had to explain your answer in words. Our kids couldn't do it, and we, as teachers, couldn't do it either. We were very frustrated. We didn't know how we were going to teach these concepts. We knew we needed help, and not just in fourth grade. We needed to have teachers teaching kids these kinds of problems from the beginning – in the earlier grades. We decided to make the whole school responsible, not just the fourth-grade teachers."

Francie continues, "It made a big difference in everyone's attitude to share the load. That's when we started to get together as a faculty. We were using the same language, and we all started to talk about our expectations. Everyone came together around the goals."

"We learned by doing it," Kit adds, "practicing and working out the problems together. All of our teachers started by using open-ended questions and grading them the same way the state grades them. We would make up problems and think about how to teach our students to solve problems. There was a good book we used to learn about how to teach problem solving, and we would take their problems and change words to get the kids' attention. We also had a lot of manipulatives, and teachers would get together and play with them. We kept practicing, and each year we got better."

To answer their action-research question definitively, Francie and her colleagues analyzed the student test scores on the Kansas Mathematics Assessment over a two-year period. Their findings corroborated their informal observations: student achievement had improved.

* This vignette is constructed from interviews with several Wilson teachers.

Each interview for this study told a story of a school built on collaboration.

While we have seen how these schools support collaborative professional learning, this central work is supported by broader shared ownership and governance of the school as a whole. Teachers work in horizontal, vertical, grade-level, or interdisciplinary teams; they serve on committees such as budget, school leadership, "campus improvement," or "test utilization"; and they participate on any number of task forces. Mason Elementary, for example, has a Student Support Team, School-Based Management Team, Instructional Leadership Team, and weekly grade-level team sessions in which teachers examine student work and look at the effects of new strategies they're trying in writing and math.

Teachers at H.D. Hilley meet weekly in horizontal grade-level teams and monthly in vertical subject-area teams that coordinate curriculum and schoolwide initiatives. Hungerford's school-based management team, which includes parents, teachers, and students, is, itself, a learning community that strives to increase students' academic success, social skills, and independent functioning. Teachers at Woodrow Wilson serve on their school's Quality Performance Accreditation committees and help shape school goals, professional development, and curricular improvements. In the same way, Montview teachers serve on a variety of committees, helping make decisions about curriculum, school resources, and new programs.

Today, shared governance is a routine practice at each of the model schools. Having a real voice in the decisions that affect them most strengthens teachers' ownership of and commitment to the change efforts. At International, a well-structured Coordinating Council handles operational and management decisions for the school. "Any major decisions are by consensus," reports one teacher:

If there is resistance — and there almost always is — people stop to ask, "How can we change it so you can live with it?" Nothing comes from the top down. New ideas or strategies are tried out by experimental teams so that buy-in from everyone is gradual and influenced by proven success. Teams and individuals are free to adapt and adjust changes to meet their own specific needs. The atmosphere here is open and trusting. Teachers are free to observe, coach, and mentor each other both individually and in team format. Their opinions are asked for and they feel valuable. They can agree or disagree, challenge and confront, take risks and make mistakes. A non-judgmental focus on the positive allows for this level of trust.

As schools build collaborative cultures in these ways, everyone comes to understand what it means to say, as one teacher does, that "School performance goals are not attained through the practices of individual teachers, but through what our faculty does as a whole." Each interview for this study told similar stories of a school built on collaboration. A "jigsaw puzzle," an H.D. Hilley teacher terms it, "where each teacher plays a role that, put together, creates magic."

What does a collegial environment look like? A teacher at Shallowford Falls offers this glimpse:

There is no competition, no superstars, because everyone is a star teacher. Everyone helps everyone else. Teachers teach for each other, share all ideas and strategies, give advice, listen, and mentor new people. It makes no difference what your role, support is always available. There are no boundaries when we work together. Everyone depends on each other. Some of the most effective staff development is what is learned from colleagues by just asking for help.

"School performance goals are not attained through the practices of individual teachers but through what our faculty does as a whole."

"That's what keeps the calmness, because everyone knows they can have their say."

The "jigsaw puzzle" mentioned earlier at Hilley is facilitated by a principal whose leadership style is to share constantly in support of a mutual vision. "This vision," one teacher explains, "started from the top and went to the bottom and then cycled back to the top in such a way that everyone was motivated to open her classroom door." A teacher at International stresses that "The voices of teachers are heard here. We feel free to offer our own ideas. And not only that — our ideas and opinions are asked for. We feel valued." A Ganado teacher concurs:

> *I think the calmness here comes from the fact that when the district went to site management, every other school had a management team. Not this school — our whole school is the team. All of us meet and talk. All of our voices are heard. That's what keeps the calmness, because everyone knows they can have their say. When decisions are made, there's buy-in because they've been heard.*

This respect for the contributions of individuals to the whole extends beyond participation in group decisions to recognition that teachers need individuality and choice in the classroom as well. While all of these schools chose some common programs to adopt, they did not interpret this to mean precise uniformity in instruction. At Montview, one teacher explains, "Even when the entire staff agrees on specific programs or techniques, individual teachers can exercise their choice in the implementation. Perhaps the success of the program lies there — in choice." Referring to individuality within group responsibility, another Montview teacher says:

> *If something is not working for a child, then it's up to the teacher to make sure it does, and use something different if necessary. At Montview, we don't just*

implement strategies, we teach children. It's important to show how it all fits in the school's goals and values along with the state standards — good, solid instruction within the parameters that have been established is the premium. As a result, teachers are not clones of each other, yet no one is out on the fringes, and there's consistency from grade level to grade level.

"The principal has to be a learner, just like every single teacher."

This interweaving of group and individual choice and accountability is often manifested in planning at multiple levels. Not only do these folks have school plans, they also have plans for teams, grade levels, or other subgroups. And, often, individual teachers write improvement plans for themselves. At Montview Elementary, for example, teachers write personal action plans that become the focus of their coaching sessions with teacher leaders. At International High School, individual core-teaching teams establish their own goals for the year as well as develop their own agendas for their meetings.

The learning community also extends beyond the teaching faculty. The principals in these schools model learning and take an active part in teacher professional development. As a Montview teacher comments, "The principal has to be a learner, just like every single teacher." In addition to participating in leadership development opportunities, these principals attend workshops and talk with the teachers about what they all are learning.

Parents, too, become part of the learning community. At H.D. Hilley, for example, parents learned technology with and from students and teachers. (See page 34, "A Place for Parents at Hilley Elementary School.")

Sometimes we were given planning time, and we were able to get more done in a couple of hours than we thought we could. There were also some staff development days, but the majority of it was after school. It was really hard to learn new things at the end of the day because we were all so tired.

— TEACHER, WOODROW WILSON

School improvement, as Fullan stresses, is about time — making time, taking time, finding more meaningful ways to spend time. Just as traditional school organization isolates teachers, so, too, is it stingy with time for working and learning together. "Caught in the crunch of inflexible time," in Phillip Schlechty's phrase, teachers and administrators feel they have little control over the way time is allocated in school. It is also one commodity — more precious even than money — that they do not have enough of: time to teach, to converse, to review student work, to develop rubrics, to create curriculum, to revise programs and policies, to know what happens in other classrooms. Many perceive time as the biggest barrier to school change. For these reasons, rethinking and restructuring time is central to building a learning culture.

Through a combination of creative planning and everyone pulling together, these award-winning schools demonstrated that they could find time to do what was needed, time both inside and outside the school day. A teacher at International High School describes the importance of teachers' scheduled time together as well the pervasiveness of on-the-fly professional conversations and learning:

Teachers' schedules are creatively arranged so that we meet — and meet often. Though the important conversations take place everywhere, from formal committees to shared rides home, putting meeting time into teachers' schedules ensures that the talking will occur.

Job-embedded coaching is possible because Title I funds are used to create time.

Schools make teachers' protected meeting and planning time available in several ways. They restructure available professional development and traditional meeting time to make it serve their goals. In some cases, they reschedule student learning time to provide extended periods for teachers to work together. Some schools use support personnel, such as substitutes, teacher assistants, student teachers, or interns, to release teachers from their classrooms so they can take part in professional development experiences. At Montview, job-embedded coaching is made possible because of the way Title I funds are used to create time — paying for classroom coverage so teachers can meet weekly with a coach, and paying for the coach position itself. (See page 24, "Coaching at Montview Elementary School.")

Faculty meetings and professional development days are restructured to get the most out of them. Rather than squandering faculty meetings on routine information that can be communicated through newsletters or e-mail, principals and teachers use this time to focus collaboratively on the "real work" of teaching. There are no more one-shot "topic du jour" presentations on inservice days, unless required by the district. In fact, there are no longer routine faculty meetings at Shallowford Falls, International High School, Montview, Hungerford, or Wilson. "We don't have faculty meetings," says a Woodrow Wilson teacher. "We're doing inservices when we get together as a staff. It's not like the day-to-day list of agenda items; you're just only talking about math."

A Place for Parents at Hilley Elementary School

When teachers at H.D. Hilley wrote the school mission statement, they specifically recognized the important role of parents as participants in the education of their children. However, because many Hilley parents are native Spanish-speakers, teachers were concerned that language barriers would discourage their participation in the life of the school.

A Challenge Grant for Technology Innovation from the U.S. Department of Education has been an important resource at Hilley for getting parents into the school and more directly involved with their children's learning. The grant funding supports new technology for classrooms, students, and parents. Hilley's on-campus Parent Center is funded by the grant and provides a place where parents can learn about technology, check out computers for use at home, and also attend adult basic education and parenting classes.

The center has become a place where teachers, students, and parents come together in a "circle of learning." For example, a resource teacher who leads the parenting classes reports, "The classes are a learning tool for me. At the same time that I am teaching the parents, I learn from them about their children – how they learn and what might help them succeed."

Another teacher, who has taught his students to tutor parents in the use of the center's computers, is proud of everyone's success: "I encourage the children to work with the parents the way I have worked with them. They are effective teachers because they can say, 'When I began, I didn't know anything, either.' We all start this as blank slates."

Best of all, as another teacher points out, "When parents are in the Parent Center, they are accessible – to the kids and to the staff."

Rescheduling the school day can free up extended blocks of time for teachers to engage in collaboration and planning. Ganado Intermediate grouped music, art, and physical education together, giving teachers a three-hour block of uninterrupted time weekly to plan with grade-level colleagues. At International High School, core-team planning time is used for professional development that teachers design themselves. At Mason, the school day starts late; teachers can get together for professional development before they meet their classes. The work other schools do in study teams, action research teams, and coaching sessions with teacher leaders is all made to fit into the school day. A few schools also use early-release days to provide teachers a one- to two-hour block of time for professional development one afternoon each week or month.

Teachers at each of these schools volunteer a tremendous amount of personal time, beyond the conventional workday, for professional development. This learning time occurs after school, before school, on weekends, and in the summer. Most of these teachers contribute one to seven hours of their own time per week for professional development.

Faculty meetings are not squandered on routine information.

Local universities offer classes at Ganado Intermediate's facility after school and also in summer. At Hungerford, teachers take part in a popular ritual — periodic Saturday professional development sessions, for which the teachers themselves determine the content. While these unique sessions are voluntary, attendance steadily increases each year. At Shallowford Falls, Ganado Intermediate, Hilley, and Montview, teachers choose to participate in after-school professional development programs available through their districts.

With stubborn resolve and ingenuity, every school creates or sets aside the time needed for staff to plan programs, exchange ideas, and reflect together about instruction, student needs, and teacher growth. This vital resource of time is indispensable for all aspects of the culture shift we've examined so far.

CHECKING FOR RESULTS

Improved job performance, changes in school organization and routines, and improved student learning are concrete indicators of the effectiveness of our professional development. Our professional development has been directed at reforming our school and improving performance of students and staff.

— TEACHER, HUNGERFORD

Perhaps the toughest challenge in schoolwide improvement is keeping the organizational eye fixed squarely on the prize. Change efforts often peter out or become sidetracked because schools are not relentless about staying the course, about sustaining momentum, about keeping their commitment alive and focused on the concrete student performance goals they set out to achieve.

Each of the these schools continually reviews programs and instructional strategies, keeping some, modifying others, discarding those that aren't working — but basing these decisions on student results, not teacher preferences. They constantly evaluate the school's professional development by one ultimate criterion: What effect is it having on kids?

In this era of accountability, such a focus on results is increasingly mandated. These schools, certainly, participate in local and state accountability programs. But for them, accountability is not just an end-of-year external requirement, it is fundamental part of the way they think about their work. As we have seen in the section on goal setting, and throughout this report, these schools focus closely on students in all they do. So for them, feedback and evaluation are ongoing.

Staying focused on results sometimes means being willing to rethink and revise.

Teachers are comfortable with multiple types of data, know how to interpret assessment results, and use available data about their students. Hungerford staff members constantly evaluate their students' progress on their IEPs. Samuel W. Mason teachers review student performance monthly, using various assessment methods. At Montview, teachers conduct in-depth quarterly assessments of their students' literacy skills. Most of these schools maintain an ongoing system of student assessment, allowing them to intervene quickly and appropriately. Frequent analysis and discussion of student work and progress — and the open nature of the professional development — enable these staffs to make mid-course corrections.

End-of-year progress reports allow school staffs to review their accomplishments and plan for the year ahead. Staying focused on results sometimes means being willing to rethink and revise. "Although solid in its design," Mason's principal says, "our professional development is far from a packaged solution. It demands continual reinvention and redirection as the Professional Development Team discovers more appropriate designs."

Just as professional development planning goes on at several levels — schoolwide, in teams, and individually — so does the stocktaking. Cross-grade teams at Shallowford Falls form goals for the school every spring based on student assessment data. Grade-level teams are given two hours of released time three times a year to develop and assess specific team goals. Each teacher also has an annual conference with the principal to discuss student achievement gains over the course of the year and achievement of individual professional development goals. As one Shallowford Falls teacher explains:

"Change is the most difficult thing — it's slow and you can lose faith — but the principal did a good job of keeping us unified."

The measure of success for staff development experiences is that students show increased scores or measurable progress on designated assessments. Teachers are accountable to show how they are using their professional learning, what they've done, and how it has made a difference for their class, their grade level, the school.

At International High School teachers participate in peer evaluation, observe each other, and develop an extensive portfolio to document progress on their professional development goals. Teachers at Montview develop action plans, which they review with teacher leaders; assessing progress is a shared responsibility.

Leadership is essential, especially through the periods of difficulty that are bound to arise. Things don't always work out as intended. Even research-based programs don't necessarily work as well or as smoothly in one site as in another. New strategies need to be tried, momentum has to be maintained, and the principal almost always plays a central role. Staff at Montview, for example, describe their principal as a leader with a vision, or as one teacher puts it:

She keeps us on the same page, going in the same direction. And because she's always working on something new, the principal models her high expectations for teacher learning.

A teacher at Mason describes her principal's efforts to keep everyone motivated and on target: "Change is the most difficult thing — it's slow, and you can lose faith — but the principal did a good job of keeping us unified. She made sure she patted us on the back and told us we were doing a good job, letting us know it will work in time, things will change — and we had to really believe that. She really kept that momentum alive."

A Boost from Outside

These schools are a triumph of the human spirit. Mostly, they succeed through their own caring and persistence. But they also benefit from help outside the school in two significant areas: pressure and support.

EXTERNAL CALL TO ACTION

It can be hard to step back from familiar routines and realize that business as usual is just not enough. Each of the eight schools in this study was spurred into greater action by a force outside of itself. In some schools, low enrollment that threatened closure was the wake-up call. For others, the appearance in local newspapers of students' state test scores sent a very public message about the school's performance. As a Wilson Elementary teacher put it, "When the state tests started to appear, that really got our attention. We're up to snuff now. That has been driving a lot of changes here." In some cases, a new principal brought higher expectations and a plan for reform. And in some of these schools a university partnership initiated a review of student performance that told a disturbing story.

External accountability measures hold schools responsible for meeting set performance standards for *all* students. In a number of model schools, these measures have caused teachers to think differently about students' capabilities. This is especially true for those teaching students with special needs. These students now have

These teachers accept responsibility for their students rather than make excuses.

more opportunities for learning because they are fully included in the classrooms or receive instruction that accommodates their needs. Their performance is now studied in light of the performance of other students. Other children who learn differently also benefit from public accountability measures. Teachers at these award-winning schools understand the unique needs of their students and are motivated to devise and adapt strategies to address them. In the words of one Mason teacher, "Now I can teach any student you give me."

What is striking about the teachers at these sites is that they accept responsibility for their students' results rather than make excuses for the results. This is a fundamental step in making change at any school.

PARTNERSHIPS WITH EXTERNAL PROGRAMS

Change really is hard. Partnerships with local universities, research-based programs, and reform networks can provide moral support, as well as material help. In these award-winning schools, help was available in some form of powerful partnership.

Ganado Intermediate, for example, has several local colleges and universities as partners. University faculty members teach on-site classes, visit the school, and serve as coaches. As a member of the rural schools network of the Bread Loaf School of English at Middlebury College in Vermont and the Northern Arizona Writing Project, Ganado has opportunities to receive training and send teachers to conferences and summer institutes. The school also participates in a Spencer Foundation grant to promote action research among rural teachers.

H.D. Hilley is a part of the Urban Systemic Initiative (USI) in its school district. The USI provides mentors to coach teachers and

Partnerships can provide moral support, as well as material help.

offers a number of workshops and training sessions for teachers in math and science. A long-term association with the University of Texas at El Paso provides research, support, and guidance about change. Several teachers at H.D. Hilley commented that their association with the university provided the fuel for change.

International High School is a member of the Annenberg New York Network for School Renewal. The collaborative gives staff members access to resources and support from other schools in the network. Several other international high schools in the New York City district are modeled after International and create a network for collaboration and inservice of teachers working with similar students and curriculum.

Samuel E. Mason Elementary maintains a number of supportive alliances. Their partnership with the John Hancock Corporation led to training in quality management in the early stages of their reform efforts. They also have partnerships with the Accelerated Schools network and City Year Youth Team, a group of young adults who help in the school. Several local colleges and universities provide other resources and expertise, from placing preservice teachers at Mason to supporting the implementation of literacy and math programs with courses and coaches.

Hungerford is part of Project Arts, a community program to bring theater and dance opportunities into the school. A few teachers, through their personal association with community groups, bring additional resources into the school to enhance their curricular areas. Teachers also tap community-based service providers to seek extra assistance and support for their special needs students.

Across the set of eight schools, teaming up with local university and college faculty brings a variety of course offerings, adds support

External Programs

A number of resources are available to help schools develop partnerships and locate research-based programs that can provide significant external assistance.

EDUCATIONAL PARTNERSHIPS PROGRAM

A Guide to Promising Practices in Educational Partnerships. Based on a national study of educational partnerships, this 63-page guide includes examples of needs assessments and strategies for staffing, staff development, community involvement, and more. Available online or from WestEd.

ed.gov/pubs/prompract/index.html/

NATIONAL STAFF DEVELOPMENT COUNCIL

Results-Based Staff Development for the Middle Grades. Twenty-six content-specific professional development programs for the middle grades are profiled online. The report can also be downloaded.

www.nsdc.org/educatorindex.htm/

NATIONAL CLEARINGHOUSE FOR COMPREHENSIVE SCHOOL REFORM

On-line services include a database of school reform research literature, funding and conference announcements, and a quarterly newsletter.

www.goodschools.gwu.edu/

NORTHWEST REGIONAL EDUCATIONAL LABORATORY

Catalog of School Reform Models. Schoolwide and content-based reform models are catalogued for on-line reading or downloading. Each model is described in terms of its origin, general description, results, implementation assistance, costs, student populations, special considerations, and selected evaluations.

www.nrel.org/scpd/natspec/catalog/

teachers, and introduces current research and information about teaching and content areas. Associations with local businesses and national networks offer these schools new perspectives, a wealth of new ideas, and access to new information. Each partnership provides expertise and access to additional opportunities for learning.

These schools are creative in locating funds to pursue their goals.

FISCAL RESOURCES

The partnerships mentioned above bring significant resources to the school: people, ideas, and concrete assistance. There's no question but that it costs money to provide people's time or material goods, or that developing and implementing ideas is expensive. Some of these partnerships are supported through state, federal, or foundation grants. Hilley, for example, benefits from mentor teachers provided via an Urban Systemic Initiative grant to the district from the National Science Foundation.

These schools draw from a wide range of funding sources for other aspects of their programs as well. They volunteer for opportunities that come up through the state or district. They seek out grants. Teachers at Hungerford wrote grants for school-based management and later sought funds to expand their innovative hydroponics unit into a three-school Web site. Several schools have technology grants. Guided by their goals for students and their improvement plans, they are creative in locating funds to pursue their goals.

But not all they do requires extensive outside funding. Some school-university partnerships are supported by the reallocation, through joint planning, of existing institutional resources of each partner — rethinking roles and relationships, not necessarily finding more money. Taking advantage of its location on the LaGuardia

Several schools arrange with local universities to host their preservice teachers, thereby expanding their professional learning community.

Community College campus, International High School shares more than facilities and resources with the college. College and high school faculty exchange some teaching assignments, and college faculty participate with the interdisciplinary teams to align high school instruction with college entry requirements. Several of the schools arrange with local universities to host their preservice teachers, thereby expanding their professional learning community.

Targeted school and district resources play their part, too. Schools have funds set aside to support teachers' attendance at off-site conferences and workshops, and although the processes for requesting these funds may differ from school to school, most teachers know that their requests are welcome if they align with school goals or their individual professional development plans. Principals and school leadership teams see that their role is to ensure adequate funding and to creatively allocate the budget to support teacher learning.

Implications for Site and District Leaders

School site leaders — both principals and teachers — played a vital role in moving these schools forward. While the lessons from these schools speak to many audiences, they are perhaps clearest for those looking to play a leadership role in their own schools. This final section draws a succinct set of actions to consider from the themes and school stories that run throughout this report.

In seven of the eight schools, the principal was a visionary leader. From cheerleading to coaching to fundraising, these principals set high expectations and provided support. They created the conditions for success, and they modeled the importance of learning in their own behavior. They also shared leadership with others on the staff, as illustrated in the section on collaborative environment. At Wilson, the primary leadership came from a core group of teachers, who initiated the math project and maintained momentum through a succession of principals. Strong leadership is critical, but it can come from a variety of sources.

The school district was not a major player in these success stories. These schools operated fairly independently from their districts. Districts provided standards and curriculum guides; they offered credit, funds, or actual opportunities to attend professional development workshops; but they were not very actively involved. In fact, several schools wished that their districts would take a more active

What Site and District Leaders Can Do

	Teachers and Principals	District Administrators
Student Data	Look at student data. Identify strengths and areas of need.	Provide data. Assist with analysis and interpretation.
Partnerships	Use external programs and partnerships to provide new ideas in areas of focus.	Help schools find external service providers and make good choices that match the school's needs.
Embedded Learning	Bring extended teacher learning opportunities and applications of new ideas into the school building. Create expectations that all will be involved in continuous professional learning related to grade-level content, and provide support for this to happen. Use principles of high-quality professional development in designing school activities. Talk to each other about teaching and learning.	Expand definitions of professional development. Find and share examples of new approaches. Consider district staff as coaches. Support the conditions that foster collaborative learning; communicate with parents and community members about what is happening and why.
Time for Collaboration	Find time for teachers to talk and work together.	Allow alternative schedules. Avoid conflicting district requirements on teachers' time.
Staffing	Expect everyone to be involved.	Assign staff to schools so as to build unity and consistency. Keep key personnel in place. Allow teachers to move out if they want.
Choice & Accountability	Allow individualization, but keep the focus on what's working for kids. Build in multiple levels of choice and accountability – school plans, grade level or team plans, individual plans.	Require site plans to focus on student needs and take into account district goals and state standards. Develop evaluation systems that are consistent with and reinforce school/individual plans.

role in promoting and supporting reform. They would like to be tapped as resources to help other schools achieve similar success.

To move from isolated examples of success — "islands of hope" as Killion terms them — to more widespread improvement, the district role becomes more important. District policies, resources, and support strategies can all help build school capacity. One way to identify more specific implications for the district's role is to map backward from the conditions we have identified in these award-winning schools. Thus, the table on page 46 suggests critical actions for both site leadership and district administrators. If school sites need to look at student data, for example, analyzing with a variety of measures what students can and cannot do, then the district's role is to help them get the data they need in a timely way and assist with analysis and interpretation. If professional development embedded in the work of the school is critical to success, then the district can help to identify, communicate, and support structures for that learning.

We hope that the suggested actions in the table, the more detailed descriptions throughout this report, and the examples of the schools themselves can inspire and guide others to follow in their footsteps.

If professional development embedded in the work of the school is critical to success, then the district can help to identify, communicate, and support structures for that learning.

Related Reading

Darling-Hammond, L., & McLaughlin, M. (1995). Policies that support professional development in an era of reform. *Phi Delta Kappan*, 76 (8), 597-604.

Outlines policy approaches consistent with goals held for teacher learning and changes in practice.

Darling-Hammond, L. & Sykes, G. (Eds.) (1999). *Teaching as the learning profession: Handbook of policy and practice.* San Francisco: Jossey-Bass.

Collects chapters by major authors on all aspects of supporting learning throughout a teacher's career.

Fullan, M. (1993). *Change forces: Probing the depths of educational reform.* London: Falmer Press.

Lays out eight basic lessons comprising a new mindset for contending with the dynamic, non-linear nature of real school change.

Lieberman, A. (1995). Practices that support teacher development: Transforming conceptions of professional learning. *Phi Delta Kappan,* 76 (8), 591-596.

Presents a broad array of strategies to support teacher learning beyond traditional professional development.

Little, J. (1999). Organizing schools for teacher learning. In Darling-Hammond, L. & Sykes, G. (Eds.) *Teaching as the learning profession: Handbook of policy and practice.* San Francisco: Jossey-Bass.

Summarizes key factors and gives examples of how schools support deep teacher learning.

Loucks-Horsley, S., Hewson, P., Love, N., & Stiles, K. (1998). *Designing professional development for teachers of science and mathematics.* Thousand Oaks, CA: Corwin Press.

Provides a framework for planning and includes in-depth descriptions of many different approaches to professional development.

Newmann, F. & Associates. (1996). *Authentic achievement: Restructuring schools for intellectual quality.* San Francisco: Jossey-Bass.

Reports on research documenting the school factors associated with student learning, including the importance of teacher professional community.

Schlechty, P. (1990). *Schools for the 21st century: Leadership imperatives for educational reform.* San Francisco: Jossey-Bass.

Approaches reform by re-examining the structure and fundamental purposes of our schools – why they are the way they are – and offers an adaptable framework for comprehensive change.

Appendix A School Profiles

Ganado Intermediate School

P.O. Box 1757
Ganado, AZ 86505
520-755-1120

Grades: 3-5

Number of Students: 515

Student Ethnicity:
99% Navajo

English Language Learners: 68%

Free/Reduced Lunch: 88%

Special Needs: 11%

Measures of Success:

- increased norm-referenced test scores
- narrowed gender achievement gap
- narrowed ELL achievement gap
- increased number of Navajo teachers
- increased parent participation

"Teachers could see a connection between what they had learned and what they were doing."

Ganado Intermediate School sits in an isolated valley on the Navajo Reservation, 30 miles west of Window Rock, Arizona. Clustered around the school are several teacher residences and two of the other three schools that make up the remote Ganado district. Almost 100 percent of the students are Navajo. Diné is their native language, and 68 percent of Ganado Intermediate School's third, fourth, and fifth graders are classified as Limited-English Proficient. For years, the Ganado students consistently scored in the lowest quartile on the state-mandated, norm-referenced tests.

Concerned for their students and energized by a new principal, the staff decided to take action. One teacher explains, "As a Navajo teacher, you feel very motivated. You know where your students are at, and you know where they need to go to have a good head start."

When Susan Stropko became principal, she had already been in the Ganado district for several years, all of them focused on supporting the district's teachers to participate in the state's professional development Career Ladder program. She was a true believer in professional development and she was knowledgeable about it. But in her initial months as principal, some other concerns came first. As she explains: " Teachers had me working hard on correcting things — there were problems in the lunch room, no soap in the bathrooms.... But by Christmas their list was getting shorter and shorter, so that by February, we were ready to say, 'What's the next step in getting this school to be the best in the state?'"

Led by the principal, teachers created a vision and a five-year plan for the school, to which they tied their own personal learning goals.

Many teachers left when they realized how determined their colleagues were to create real change. The teachers who stayed and those who chose to come to Ganado Intermediate found that while many resources, such as ESL classes and other university courses, were already available on site through Career Ladder, many more were needed if they were to address the goals they were setting for their students' learning.

Among the learning opportunities brought in to address teacher-identified needs were CLIP (Collaborative Literature Intervention Project), Northern Arizona Writing Project, a Spencer Foundation project on teacher inquiry, Foundations of Learning (Navajo culture and philosophy of education), and Integrated Thematic Instruction.

The district was generous in providing on-site, free coursework and giving teachers credit for it on the pay scale. The principal both nudged and encouraged teachers and teaching assistants to participate in these learning opportunities. And the staff appreciated these resources. "I've never been in a district with so many professional development opportunities," more than one teacher notes.

Nonetheless, teachers recognized that just taking courses was not enough. They wanted time together, to talk about what they were learning and to see how it was playing out with their students. So the school schedule was reconfigured with "allied" subjects like art and physical education grouped for each grade. This gave grade-level teams a solid block of time to meet every week to focus on student learning — to assess their students' work and progress and to determine what they, as teachers, needed to do or learn to become more effective with their kids.

The result, as the principal reports, was that "I could ask teachers what they were doing with a particular child and they could trace back to what had influenced them and see a connection between what they had learned and what they were doing."

In addition to grade-level meetings, Ganado Intermediate staff met every other week as a whole group — teachers, administrators, part-time teacher helpers, and teaching assistants. Teachers had decided that rather than send representatives to a school management team, they would all meet and make decisions about their school together. The principal often brought student scores to the group, to help focus decisions about what to do next.

The sense of the whole school as a learning community reinforced a goal held by the Navajo Nation as well as the school. That goal was to increase the number of Navajo teachers by supporting the teacher helpers and teaching assistants — all members of the local Navajo community — to take courses that would lead to a teaching credential. Currently 40 percent of the faculty is Navajo, and several new teachers have come out of this support system. The principal who has now replaced Stropko is Navajo, as well.

Negotiating cultural differences has been part of the learning at the school. One non-Navajo teacher notes, "We've had to learn about ourselves, our different learning styles, and our different ways of handling things — basic differences like whether interrupting is supportive or rude, whether long conversational pauses are seen as time to think." A Navajo teacher adds, "We have to understand our Native American students, and especially we have to understand their code switching and not label them deficient or limited."

When teachers talk together about students, they have learned to appreciate that their Navajo and Anglo perspectives may be different but that their goals for the students are the same. "Teamwork" comes up a lot when teachers describe the highlights of their Ganado experience.

When Ganado Intermediate received a National Award for Model Professional Development, the effectiveness of their teamwork was recognized. "That was major," says Lucinda Swedburg, a former Ganado teacher who is the new principal. "We proudly display it, on everything. I just wish the words said, 'For Student Achievement,' because that's why we did it in this building."

H.D. Hilley Elementary School

693 N. Rio Vista Road
El Paso, TX 79927
915-860-3770

Grades: K-5

Number of Students: 690

Student Ethnicity:
- 89% Latino
- 11% White
- 1% African American

English Language Learners: 24%

Free/Reduced Lunch: 70%

Special Needs: 9%

Measures of Success:
- 1997 Texas Successful School
- increased state assessment scores

"We all know what everyone else is doing."

When principal Ivonne Durant first arrived at H.D. Hilley Elementary School, she and the staff decided to upset some stereotypes about who can learn. The state test scores said Hilley students couldn't. But instead of making excuses for their students, whose homes are among the cotton fields of rural Texas and whose demographics as poor and Latino often add up to school failure, the school got focused. Several teachers left. And now everyone knows what the goals are and what is expected — for staff and students.

After only two years, Hilley was chosen by the Texas Education Agency as a "Texas Successful School," in recognition of the impressive progress students were making.

"We are motivated by each other," says a teacher who appreciates the transition the school has been able to make. "Before, I was doing my own writing program, my own reading program. Now I am doing what the whole school is doing. It is easier for the teachers. We all know what everyone else is doing. Now we are more directed."

This direction comes from many levels. An evaluator meets with the staff at the beginning of the year to help them analyze their students' needs and decide how to meet them. Teachers and administrators are aware throughout the year of how well they are meeting their goals. "We all give ourselves pressure," says one teacher. "We tell each other what we expect." At the end of the year, everyone sits down again to analyze what the state test scores tell them about where they can improve.

In addition to the leadership of the School Improvement Team of parents, community members, teachers, and administrators, Hilley's vertical teams, which include teacher representatives from each grade level, coordinate learning in key content areas. Teams for communications, mathematics and science, fine arts, and technology (which has now been integrated into the other three areas) meet with the principal for a half day every other month, making recommendations for whole-school professional development. "I like the way we break into the vertical teams," says one teacher. "We become specialists in that area. It makes you want to stay abreast, keep up."

The vertical teams also cross-fertilize the horizontal, grade-level teams, which meet for an hour each week. As a first-grade teacher reports, "In our grade levels we get together every single week and strategize what is working and not working." Minutes from their meetings keep the principal informed of particular issues that come up, and she is a frequent observer in classrooms, noting how teachers use what they are learning.

The assistant principal and literacy mentor are additional resources to teachers, observing, providing demonstration lessons, debriefing with them, and participating in the informal learning that is pervasive in the building. As the mentor points out, "We do a lot of sharing. We make the time, even if it is just a short moment walking down the hall, even in the bathrooms. We e-mail each other. If you find an article that is related to what someone else is doing, you put it in their box. I have books in my room that are borrowed from everyone. We are constantly aware of what everyone is doing."

Technology has been a major push at Hilley, with the school's participation in the district Technology Innovation Challenge Grant from the U.S. Department of Education providing computers and training for the school. Teachers really do e-mail each other. And students, from first grade on up, use computers for anything from word processing to HyperStudio presentations. Parents have also been encouraged to learn and teach each other how to use the new technology. Computers are always available to them in the school's Parent Center.

Finally, collaboration and alliances with partner organizations are a feature of Hilley staff's continuous learning. Through partnerships arranged by the Socorro School District, teachers at Hilley can study for tuition-free Master's degrees, enroll in a two-year technology specialty, take advantage of mentors funded by the National Science Foundation, and benefit from the revamped teacher education program at the University of Texas at El Paso. University student teachers and education school faculty are a regular source of new ideas for the school. As principal Durant reports, "The role of the university is huge, huge. Both for degrees and for our training. They are a key ingredient of our professional development." All of this has translated into improved academic achievement for the Hilley students, students that Durant and her staff members proudly refer to as *mijos* and *mijas*.

Hungerford School

P.S. 721R
155 Tompkins Avenue
Staten Island, NY 10304
718-273-8622

Grades: 12 to 21 years old

Number of Students: 250

Student Ethnicity:

- 59% White
- 20% African American
- 15% Latino
- 6% Asian

English Language Learners: 14%

Free/Reduced Lunch: 67%

Special Needs: 100%

Measures of Success:

- more students use technology
- increased job placements
- more students achieve IEPs
- more students included in general education

"People are encouraged to run with their strengths."

Any morning before school, the parking lot outside Hungerford School provides a dramatic introduction to this remarkable place. Students arrive by ambulances, handicap-equipped buses and vans, and private cars. Nurses and physical therapists join the teachers and paraprofessionals who make their way inside to serve Hungerford's special needs students, many of whom are classified as medically fragile and severely to profoundly retarded. While a number of students enter the building in wheelchairs, on crutches, or on gurneys, 100 of the 250 12- to 21-year-old students will soon be on their way to work-study placements at businesses and agencies around their Staten Island community.

At Hungerford, these special students have attracted a special staff. Faculty turnover is low, but when new teachers are hired, they often have previously been paraprofessionals in the school. Staff voluntarily give up six Saturdays a year to learn about topics of their choosing, from CPR, to new educational technology, to special arts programming. The Saturday atmosphere is homey, as teachers' children filter through the school building, free to work on the school computers or watch videos rented by the PTA. Food is provided for everyone, and the men do the cooking. Attendance at these gatherings has grown over the years from under a third to an impressive 80 percent of the staff.

The collegiality reflected in these voluntary sessions is also apparent in teachers' weekly team meetings. Instead of typical faculty meetings, teachers attend meetings of staff committees that function as self-directed professional development teams. The teams focus on technology, literacy, math/science, arts, behavior management, and school-to-work transition, and they establish standards for students in each area.

Each team is free to set its own agenda, tied to goals for students. They may request funds to have experts come in, or conduct their own action research, or create curriculum or alternative assessments appropriate for Hungerford students. One team's action research, for example, found that students in group homes gained more weight than other students. The result was a program to get Hungerford students actively participating in the community gym program where students had been placed for work-study. Another team wrote a successful grant to extend a teacher-developed unit about hydroponics into a three-school Web site where students communicate about what they are learning.

Parents are surveyed as well for ideas about professional development efforts that might help their children, and they are active members of the school-based management team.

Individually, too, teachers participate in a wide variety of professional development opportunities — at the district level, as well as at the school. These range from off-site courses and visits to other schools, to on-site lunchtime meetings with other teachers and visits to each other's classrooms. "There is a lot of fluidity in the building," reports a 10-year veteran. "Teachers go into each other's classrooms. Every student is everybody's student. We're thinking constantly about preparing our students for life."

Teachers' commitment to their students is documented in the professional development portfolios they keep. No matter how teachers choose to invest their professional development time and energy, the portfolio helps them reflect on everything they are learning and how it relates to the school's overall goals for students. The results include an increase in the number of Hungerford students able to use technology, placed in community-based work sites, achieving their individual educational plan goals, and participating in general education classes.

"Nine years ago," says Principal Mary McInerney, "when the state first called for school-based management, a group of teachers wrote and received a grant to begin learning how to go about it. We met regularly and they took ownership, surveying the rest of the staff about their interests in learning."

Teachers are still in charge of their own learning at Hungerford. They participate annually in discussions about where to focus, and the professional development budget is open to everyone. "We haven't had to turn down any requests yet," McInerney notes.

This openness and flexibility on the part of the principal pays off for Hungerford faculty and their students. As one long-time teacher observes, "There is lots of communication. Our principal knows her people, knows their strengths. Two weeks ago I got notice of a grant I wanted to apply for. She got me the support I need to write a grant proposal for the school. She encourages people to run with their strengths."

International High School at LaGuardia Community College

31-10 Thomson Avenue	
Long Island City, NY 11101	
718-482-5482	
Grades: 9-12	
Number of Students: 450	
Student Ethnicity:	
45%	Latino
30%	Asian
22%	White
2%	African American
English Language Learners: 73%* (37 different languages)	
Free/Reduced Lunch: 82%	
Special Needs: 0%	
Measures of Success: • increased graduation rates • increased attendance rates • increased college acceptance rates • narrowed ELL achievement gap	

*100% of students are admitted as English Language Learners.

"With this level of decision-making power, we have very, very few excuses for not doing the job."

Students can only be admitted to International High School in the New York City district if their English language skills are in the bottom 20 percent citywide and they have been in this country for fewer than four years. It is an admissions test that most students in New York might wish they could pass. At International, students beat the district average in course pass rates, four-year graduation rates, and retention rates (only 1.7 percent drop out of high school, compared with 16.4 percent districtwide). Over 90 percent of International graduates are accepted into college.

Several years ago, the teachers at International found students' limited English language ability to be a persuasive reason to organize the school into small teams and to organize the curriculum for interdisciplinary depth. "A couple of experimental teams were formed," one teacher explains, "and their students were getting better results, doing more sophisticated work. As a school, we decided, okay, this is the way we're going to go."

Now, six teams of six teachers each have extraordinary authority to manage the education of their particular 75 students for the year. "I'm amazed at how much power is given to teams to make decisions," says a teacher who came to International after 17 years in other schools. Another teacher points out the corollary, "It's wonderful," she says, "but you see the problem — there are no excuses. With this level of decision-making power, we have very, very few excuses for not doing the job."

"The job" that teachers do begins not in their classrooms, but in their teams.

Each team meets three hours a week, to develop and revise their interdisciplinary curriculum, share successful practices and troubleshoot problems, allocate a team budget, hire and mentor new teachers for the team, and discuss, or case manage, individual students.

If students are having trouble, International does not have a dean's office to send them to. Kids belong to the team. A third-year teacher explains, "We all see the same kids, and when there's a problem with a kid, it's everybody's problem. You can imagine, especially for a new teacher, how wonderful that is. Case management is a great way to make sure kids don't fall through the cracks."

Teachers don't fall through the cracks either. In addition to the support of team members, new teachers often find themselves team teaching their first year. A new teacher reports, "Things that it takes years and years of teaching to do well, I learned from watching my master teacher and from her feedback."

Additional support, in the form of peer evaluation, occurs annually for teachers' first two years at International and then every third year. "It is an opportunity for us to showcase what we're doing, to ask for help solving problems, and to find out what other teachers are doing," says one teacher. "All that opening up and talking to other people has dramatically changed how I teach," adds another teacher who had felt isolated in other schools.

Teachers also write self-evaluations and create professional portfolios. According to a teacher in her sixth year of teaching, "It gives me a chance to synthesize what I've done, put it together in a coherent way, and focus on my next goals."

When the staff saw how powerful portfolios were for their own learning, the teams started to move away from student tests toward having students show their work to each other and discuss it. Monthly staff meetings, as well as team meetings, have focused on how to institute graduation projects or portfolios. This has meant creating and aligning rubrics with the state standards and graduation requirements. It has also meant supporting students in every class so that by the time they are seniors, they're each prepared to create a successful portfolio.

Teachers, who personally advise several seniors apiece, acknowledge how much work implementing the portfolio process has been, but also how valuable it is, for teachers as well as students. Says one teacher, "I can't overemphasize how important this has been and how much we learn from it."

"The key to school reform is learning," says principal Eric Nadelstern. "All new learning creates change. If your goal for students is to show that education can transform your life, you must have a school culture that demonstrates that adults are capable of learning. We model a structure where teachers can learn."

Samuel W. Mason Elementary School

150 Norfolk Avenue
Roxbury, MA 02119
617-635-8405

Grades: K-5

Number of Students: 300

Student Ethnicity:
- 71% African American
- 14% White
- 11% Latino
- 2% Asian
- 2% Native American

English Language Learners: 23%

Free/Reduced Lunch: 74%

Special Needs: 26%

Measures of Success:
- doubled enrollment
- went from 79th most-chosen to 12th most-chosen school in district
- almost doubled districtwide test score gains

"This school's professional development began with the inclusion children."

Before a new principal arrived in 1990, the Boston School District was ready to shut Samuel W. Mason Elementary School down and lock the doors. Of the 79 elementary schools in the district, parents chose "The Mason," as it is called, dead last.

"With that sense of urgency," former principal Mary Russo explains, "we had to take a tough look at our school." The school's Roxbury neighborhood was itself a tough one, but that wasn't going to change. What had to change was that reading scores were in the lowest quartile in the district and that teachers were operating in total isolation.

Starting essentially from scratch, the school community needed a vision for the school. Parents were asked, "What kind of school do you want your kids to go to?" Teachers were asked, "What kind of school would you want *your* kids to go to? And the kids were asked, "What would a good school look like to you?"

The next question was how to provide the resources to make the changes everyone agreed were needed. One key decision was to become a total inclusion school. This meant the special education teachers and paraprofessionals would be resources for the whole school. Classroom teachers would absorb the special education students, but there would be more teachers to go around. (The school later became a professional development site for the special education program at Wheelock College, with Wheelock students augmenting the school's contingent of paraprofessionals.)

Total inclusion also made it dramatically clear that the whole school would have to think about educating children in a different way. In one teacher's opinion, "This school's professional development began with the inclusion children. To have special needs kids in your class, to have a diverse range of achievement levels in your room, you have to be a more careful observer, and you have to be a better problem solver about your methods."

Another teacher concurs: "I've been teaching for 32 years, and education has changed so much. In the past if Johnny didn't learn it was Johnny's problem. But now, if he didn't learn, there's something you're not doing. I think special education has done a lot to clarify our views on education in general — it's up to us to find optimal conditions for a child to learn."

This change in attitude about responsibility for children's learning was reinforced through the school's decisions to become one of the Boston district's first school-based management sites and to join the Accelerated Schools Network. The district provided a "change coach" and Accelerated Schools delivered the message that not only can all children learn, but children who are behind can learn enough to catch up.

The Mason also needed to find a literacy program that would pull everyone together. "It was always isolated pockets for years," one teacher explains. "There was no syllabus, no dialogue about when to teach what, no common language or goals."

After investigating and visiting various programs, the School-Based Management Team recommended Early Literacy Learning Initiative (ELLI). Parents and faculty then took a hard look at it, finally agreeing to implement it. Teachers credit much of their learning to ELLI and the fact that a Mason teacher is an on-site, half-time demonstration teacher and coach in the program.

Teachers are also free to visit and coach each other since the school's paraprofessionals, student teachers, and parent volunteers can step in to cover for them. "We have the mentality that you learn from seeing others," reports one teacher. "If someone says they tried something and it went really well, we'll all say, 'Can we see it?'"

Under new principal Jane Palmer Owens, many professional development activities at The Mason are built into the school day. Classes don't start until 9:20, which means that some kind of professional development is going on every morning in the building. Grade-level teams meet weekly. Other teams meet with a focus on literacy or math or site-based management. And a Student Support Team meets twice a month to keep close track of kids who are having trouble or could benefit from special services.

In addition to the schoolwide goals for professional development, teachers have personal goals that they discuss twice a year with the principal. The Mason teachers now average 50 hours of professional development each, up from 6 hours in 1991.

As for student learning, the fact that all professional development is tightly aligned with student assessments has paid off. Twice a month, grade-level teams meet to go over student work. Three times a year, teachers formally assess their students and make presentations to the faculty and parents. And, of course, there are the standardized tests required by the district. On recent tests of reading, math, and writing, The Mason students outperformed the district average in every case, posting gains that have made their school one of the 12 most desirable in Boston, as determined by the parents who vote every day to send their children there.

Montview Elementary School

2055 Moline Street
Aurora, CO 80010
303-364-8549
Grades: K-5
Number of Students: 860
Student Ethnicity:
46% Latino
27% African American
21% White
5% Asian
1% Native American
English Language Learners: 42%
Free/Reduced Lunch: 77%
Special Needs: 13%
Student Transiency: 126%

Measures of Success:

- increased reading and math scores from below to above district average
- virtually eliminated ethnicity performance gaps
- selected as Literacy Learning Network demonstration site

"We can articulate why we're doing what we're doing."

As the student population at Montview shifted from suburban to urban, as the number of English language learners skyrocketed, and as the transiency rate topped 100%, the staff made a choice — to focus on how children learn, to equip themselves with research-based teaching strategies, and to embed professional development in the day-to-day life of the school. Some teachers transferred out when the demands became clear, but others transferred in. "In the years before I came to Montview, I was a so-so teacher, but it was important for me to continually develop. I made a choice to come here because of the professional development, and I've never felt so supported."

Rather than perseverate on their students as "at-risk" learners, the staff decided to clarify their beliefs about learning, and then apply them. They began by choosing an established staff development program, the Literacy Learning Network, to implement schoolwide.

The structure set up five years ago to support that implementation is still in place. Title I funds are used to release selected staff members from classroom duties so that they can function as coaches, or "teacher leaders," for other staff. Each leader has a group of teachers he or she observes once a week.The leader then meets individually with each one to discuss the observation and to help the teacher update or make adjustments to his or her personal action plan.

In addition to the concrete, classroom-specific learning promoted through these coaching relationships, nearly all the staff attend Wednesday "dialogue" sessions to bring research resources and professional articles to bear on schoolwide learning issues.Teachers earn district credit for attending these voluntary after-school sessions, participate in preparing the agendas, and facilitate the dialogue.

According to teachers, this model works because they think of themselves as learners in the same way they think about their students as learners — as being on a continuum, always ready to take the next step.They are all expected to generate questions about what they are doing, what they are learning, and what they would like to try or find out.

"My action plans," explains a third-year teacher, "began the first year looking at the literacy model, since I was not familiar with it. Then my coach would suggest things and I was able to deepen those understandings. Now, this year, I am directed by my own questions, things I wonder about from talking with other staff members or my grade level."

Relatively new teachers aren't the only ones who thrive in this atmosphere. As a veteran teacher points out, "Because each of us works on an individualized action plan, which is very relevant and very real, it is hard to get burned out. You are always being challenged by some kind of new learning. It would be hard to get stuck in a rut."

Principal Debbie Backus would agree that she, too, is learning a lot. "The heart of all we're doing here," she says, "is developing theories to support our practice." One way Backus builds her professional understanding is through the Wednesday dialogue sessions. As one teacher observes, "I really respect the fact that she comes to our dialogues. She's so professional we want to attend." Adds another teacher, "She understands what an instructional leader does. She is a learner just like every single teacher. She works on action plans. She had to learn herself how kids learn. She is always working on something new."

"Originally," Backus reports, "professional development came from the teacher evaluation process, but when we started letting student assessment drive instruction, using data about our kids, it changed our professional development orientation to understanding the learner, to really understanding what do you know about the student.

"Our professional development is job-embedded, focused on real problems and real issues, with teachers feeling they have strategies, ways to deal with why a kid is learning or not learning. Talk in this school is professional. We can articulate why we're doing what we're doing."

What Montview staff are doing has paid off for students in both reading and math. Students' scores on standardized tests moved from below the district average to the top of the district range. In addition, teachers have been able to virtually eliminate ethnic performance gaps. But as one teacher describes success, "I'm successful when I open the door and 99 percent of the kids show up, even when the weather is crummy, even when they don't feel well, because they want to be there."

Shallowford Falls Elementary School

3529 Lassiter Road
Marietta, GA 30062
770-640-4815

Grades: K-5

Number of Students: 660

Student Ethnicity:
- 90% White
- 3% African American
- 3% Latino
- 3% Asian

English Language Learners: 0.5%

Free/Reduced Lunch: 3%

Special Needs: 15%

Measures of Success:
- steadily higher ITBS scores even with baseline scores above district average
- selected as Talents Unlimited demonstration site

"We're all focusing on the same thing. Nothing comes out of left field somewhere."

In 1990, Shallowford Falls Elementary was a brand new school, built to serve a prosperous Atlanta suburb. Parents' expectations were high, but they couldn't have imagined that the principal's and teachers' expectations were even higher. Principal Cheryl Hunt Clements interviewed 250 teachers before selecting her staff, and she made it clear what the demands would be. As one teacher puts it, "You've got to be willing to give 112 percent. From the moment we got here, Cheryl expressed the idea that everyone would be a team player."

Over the years, through site-based management, teachers have decided to focus that 112 percent on improving students' scores on the Iowa Test of Basic Skills (ITBS) — in a school where students already score well above the district average. "It's such a big job," one teacher explains, "that you can't do it alone. We have to think of ourselves as a team."

As evidence of this team approach, no matter what students' test percentiles are in first and second grade, by fifth grade they're higher. The gains are cumulative across the grades. In fact, Shallowford Falls fifth graders are consistently the highest in the district.

Each spring, a cross-grade team analyzes the new ITBS scores to draft the School Improvement Plan and associated professional development plan for the year ahead. Those plans are shared with the whole staff, reviewed by the principal, and reviewed again by the staff. "It's bottom up and then comes back down and we refine it," says one teacher. "In the end, it's mandatory, but we're all focusing on the same thing. Nothing comes out of left field somewhere."

In addition to the schoolwide goals, grade-level teams and individual teachers also have score-driven goals. The principal sees her role in helping teachers use their test data as crucial to the process. "Every year," she explains, "we rank ourselves by each sub-test against each of the 61 elementary schools in the district. Each grade level identifies its strengths and weaknesses." For example, one year the student gains for the whole fourth grade were low in listening skills, so improving the teaching of listening skills became a focus for that team.

Grade-level teams are given release time three times a year to analyze their students' strengths and weaknesses. They also meet after school one Thursday a month, and they get together informally at lunch or whenever they need help or want to share a success. A veteran teacher explains, "The greatest resource you have is the teacher next door. That's really practiced here." Another teacher cites the example of the first year she taught third grade: "My scores were the lowest in third grade, so I went to the teacher that had the highest scores. The next year I copied what she did, and my class scores came up."

Teachers analyze their own weaknesses and write personal goals that are shared with their grade-level team and the principal — not as mea culpas but for support. As one teacher unabashedly reveals, "What I need to beef up this year is more language and punctuation. Ten of my kids went down, so that's a personal thing I can improve on to help the kids. I assumed they knew more than they did. But something got missed."

Teachers also develop goals for each student, which they go over with the principal. The principal explains, "We develop a profile sheet for each student, over time, from grade to grade, and it specifies for each child how much to push. At the end of the year we also look at each child's gain scores and try to figure out, if any child did exceptionally well, why, and if a child didn't do well, why. That information is passed on to the child's next teacher."

All this focus is relentless. Says one teacher, "We put the kids under a microscope, but they can tell you how much their personal score has gone up, and they can see their growth."

After school, the focus widens and students have a wide range of activities such as art, drama, Spanish, and running clubs to help them develop more broadly.

Parents at Shallowford Falls are highly involved in their children's school experience. Between 90 and 100 percent of them turn out for the many events planned for parents, and they also show up to help out. "The involvement of parents," one teacher points out, "has been a huge part of our success. As teachers, we learn and do our thing, and the kids need to do their thing, too. Homework and class work are not optional. The parents know that and they are supportive."

Woodrow Wilson Elementary School

312 N. Juliette Avenue
Manhattan, KS 66502
913-587-2170

Grades: K-6

Number of Students: 320

Student Ethnicity:

80%	White
15%	African American
3%	Asian
1%	Latino
1%	Native American

English Language Learners: 1%

Free/Reduced Lunch: 44%

Special Needs: 30%

Measures of Success:

- increased student performance in math
- increased student performance in science
- increased student performance in reading and language arts

"One of the things we have going for us is that each staff development builds on the last one. They all fit together."

Woodrow Wilson Elementary School and its mostly veteran faculty members had a long association with Kansas State University well before the new state math assessments left their students high and dry. That connection continues now that the school and university have restructured professional development so that not only math, but also reading, writing, and science scores have shot up.

"It goes back to the '80s," reports a teacher who's been there long enough to know. During that time many Wilson teachers took courses at the university and participated in university projects and summer programs. One of those projects was to help the university restructure its program for preservice teachers. "It was very motivating," says this same long-time Wilson teacher, "going to the university, meeting with educators at that level, and being empowered to be experts."

Following the evolution of the university's preservice program, Wilson was tapped to become one of its professional development schools, and the association with KSU deepened. As another Wilson veteran observes, "Being a PDS school provides us with a lot of opportunities — to take classes for credit or stipends, to go to workshops, to participate in grants." But it wasn't until she and two of her colleagues took an action-research course, that the university-school relationship really took off.

The "course" coincided with the embarrassing math problem-solving scores for Wilson students, and it led to a new approach to professional development for the whole school. "Those three [teachers] focused us in," acknowledges one of their colleagues. "They were in the math area, looking at the state assessment, and they identified some areas where our kids needed to improve. They were the pioneers."

Originally, the principal gave up two faculty meetings a month for the whole staff to participate in the math action-research effort. Teachers took the math assessment themselves, figured out what their kids were going to need to know, wrote practice math problems for students to work with, and scored and analyzed real student responses to real test items. "I don't think of it as having to teach to the test," one teacher says. "It's caused our teaching to be what it should be."

Teachers still meet twice a month, in addition to their district staff development days. The focus for these meetings, which are faculty-led, is decided at the beginning of the year by a faculty committee in response to colleagues' suggestions and student needs. As one teacher explains, "Now all these things are in the fire, inservice-wise. People say, 'Maybe we need that kind of emphasis in reading or social studies.' The whole staff is infected."

But it is the *structure* of the professional development, more than any particular content area, that really seems to make the difference for Woodrow Wilson teachers. "Before," a teacher admits, "you could go to an inservice and not really do anything because there was no follow-up. Now we're always back talking within a month because of something we did together. Sometimes I get disorganized, but this kind of inservice drives you, keeps you on course." Another teacher concurs, "One of the things we have going for us is that each staff development builds on the last one. They all fit together."

For one of the few new teachers to join the Wilson faculty, this structure proved especially helpful. "The inservices had a momentum, it was ongoing learning. I just glided in," she says.

In addition to the learning that teachers do with their colleagues, over 50 preservice students are in the building each semester, with about 10 of them doing their student teaching, while the others come in with a specific content-area focus. This level of interaction with teacher candidates makes it easy for even the most jaded of teachers to embody the adage that the best way to learn is to teach.

"We've changed the way we see preservice teachers here," one of the senior staff members explains. "Our teachers don't just turn their class over. We've really pushed the team-teaching, cooperative approach. Our teachers explain what they're doing to the preservice teachers. And while they're doing that, they're thinking through and justifying what they're doing. The preservice teachers are very open, like sponges, about learning. But because they're also in some ways critiquing what they see, the classroom teachers are doing their best job every day."

Despite frequent turnover in the principalship at Wilson, the staff has moved ahead, taking responsibility for its own professional development, working with the university, and implementing a number of curricular and instructional changes to support increased student achievement. Notes one teacher, "We've had a rotation of principals through here. I have to give a lot of credit to the staff."

Appendix B The Research Study

When the U.S. Department of Education contracted with WestEd to conduct a study of eight schools that received department awards for their professional development programs, the first question to answer was *What teacher learning opportunities are available in these schools?* Next, the study asked *How do teachers learn in these schools?* These broad questions naturally suggested other questions: What is the structure of the professional development programs? What human and financial resources support ongoing learning? What are the roles of the principal, teachers, and district? and What is the context in which continuous improvement occurs?

Under contract to WestEd, Joellen Killion of the National Staff Development Council designed and managed a process to answer these and related questions. (The initial research report is available at www.WestEd.org/wested/news.html/.) The first step was to create teacher and principal interview protocols designed to help identify the multiple factors that contributed to success in these schools.

Next, eight researchers were selected for their expertise in professional development and/or evaluation. Team members, regardless of their background, took part in interview training and training in methods of data collection and data analysis.

Then a two-member site team visited each school for two days. During the two days, the site team conducted in-depth interviews with 3 to 6 teachers and the principal. Brief interviews were also conducted with 4 to 13 more teachers. In some cases, to accommodate teachers' schedules, group interviews were held at lunchtime and within team meetings. For two of the three schools that had had new principals since the school was recognized, both the former principal and the current principal were interviewed.

In total, site teams conducted 30 in-depth teacher interviews (60-90 minutes), 64 brief teacher interviews (30 minutes), and 10 principal interviews (60-90 minutes) between mid-May and late June 1999. Despite hectic schedules at the end of the school year, teachers, students, principals, and support staff graciously welcomed the researchers and eagerly shared their stories.

Data collected by each team were analyzed and compiled using a domain analysis process, which allowed the researchers to group similar data from the different schools and to characterize factors that appeared to be important across the eight schools' diverse settings and circumstances.

Analysis of these factors was the major reason for conducting this study. But interview data can yield much more. Data from interviews were also used to develop a number of vignettes and the site profiles in Appendix A. In addition, direct quotes from teachers and principals have been included generously in this report to convey the very real energy and effort behind the data.

Many, many teachers were interviewed, more than were necessary simply to "get the story." What we also wanted this report to reflect was what happened for *most* teachers in these schools, to represent the voice of "every teacher." This is not to say that these are "ordinary" teachers. They are all, in fact, extraordinary. They worked outside their comfort zones. They came together and made decisions to influence the direction of the entire school. They set aside their personal interests for the benefit of their students, working hard and long. They supported and coached one another in a community of learners. And they demanded the best of themselves and their colleagues. Their individual views and collective experience can instruct us all.

MATRES LECTIONIS
IN ANCIENT HEBREW EPIGRAPHS

by
Ziony Zevit

Published by
AMERICAN SCHOOLS OF ORIENTAL RESEARCH

Distributed by

AMERICAN SCHOOLS OF ORIENTAL RESEARCH
126 Inman Street
Cambridge, MA 02139

MATRES LECTIONIS IN ANCIENT HEBREW EPIGRAPHS

by

Ziony Zevit

Cover design by Suellen Feinberg

Library of Congress Cataloging in Publication Data

Zevit, Ziony.
Matres lectionis in ancient Hebrew epigraphs.

(Monograph series - American Schools of Oriental Research; no. 2)

Bibliography: p. 37.
1. Hebrew language—Orthography and spelling. 2. Hebrew language—Vocalization. 3. Inscriptions, Hebrew—Palestine. I. Title. II. Series: American Schools of Oriental Research. Monograph Series - American Schools of Oriental Research; no. 2.
PJ4583.Z4 492.4'152 80-19652
ISBN 0-89757-402-8

Printed in the United States of America

To the memory of my grandfather, a student and a scholar, Ben-Zion, the son of Aharon Yosef Zwet, who would have understood that it too is *talmūd Tōrāh*.

Preface

During the ten years in which I have been engaged in this project, there has been an increasingly rapid rate of change and progress in what once was considered a relatively somnifacient discipline: ancient Hebrew epigraphy. Just as the availability of new data stimulated this undertaking, and just as new discoveries and publications delayed its completion, so additional discoveries will eventually necessitate modification, amplification, and revision of its conclusions at one or more points.

In the decade during which it has evolved from a few pages of critical notes into its present form, this monograph has benefited from the encouragement, advice, and criticism of many individuals. Thanks are due to A. Bloch (University of California at Berkeley), with whom I discussed phonological and syntactic problems in the late sixties; D. N. Freedman (University of Michigan), with whom I briefly discussed problems relating to stress and orthography also in the late sixties; J. Blau (Hebrew University), Sh. Morag (Hebrew University), and S. Gevirtz (Hebrew Union College), who read and commented on the antepenultimate draft of this study; Z. Meshel (Tel-Aviv University), who corresponded with me about the Kuntilet ᶜAjrud materials before their official publication; A. Rainey (Tel-Aviv University), with whom I discussed the Arad and Beer-Sheba excavations and ostraca; and D. Owen (Cornell University), who shared with me information concerning a tablet discovered in the 1978 excavations at Aphek, inscribed in what may be a new Canaanite script.

Above all, thanks are due to J. C. Greenfield (Hebrew University), who, as my advisor, teacher, and friend, oversaw the growth of this work through 1973 and who since then has drawn my attention to relevant new discoveries and publications before this knowledge was disseminated in the American academic market place. My fascination with Hebrew epigraphy is directly traceable to the infectious excitement with which he filled his graduate seminar on Canaanite dialects at The University of California at Berkeley.

D. Lieber, President of the University of Judaism, provided a subvention to defray a portion of the printing costs, and D. Gordis, Director of the University College of Jewish Studies, freed the time of N. Brunswick and B. Leebolt to work on the typescript. These took great pains and demonstrated even greater grace in typing and retyping the final draft as well as a number of mini-revisions which new publications necessitated. L. Shub, Director of the University Library, diplomatically refrained from mentioning the library budget while okaying the acquisition of some exorbitantly priced volumes which I used in preparing this study. S. Spiro, my congenial research assistant during the 1978-79 academic year, rendered invaluable help in preparing the final draft for publication. To all of these who made life in the ivory tower so pleasant, I am grateful.

Finally, I dedicate this work to the memory of my grandfather, a student and a scholar, Ben-Zion, the son of Aharon Yosef Zwet, who would have understood that it too is *talmūd Tōrāh.*

TABLE OF CONTENTS

Page

Chapter I
The Study of *Matres Lectionis*

Ever since the pioneering studies of Wilhelm Gesenius in 1837 attempted to apply data derived from Phoenician inscriptions to questions posed by the inconsistent orthography of the Hebrew Bible, scholars have returned periodically to investigate the problem anew (Miller 1927: 18; Cross and Freedman 1952: 1-10).[1] The objective of these investigations has been to describe how, when, and why the graphemes ʾ*alep*, *he*, *waw*, and *yod* came to be used as vowel indicators in addition to their use as consonant indicators. Although some medieval Jewish scholars had already speculated the employment of these four graphemes as *matres lectionis* (hereafter, *m.l.*) to be a late development in Hebrew orthography,[2] it was only with the discovery and study of Phoenician, Moabite, Aramaic, and Hebrew inscriptions from Syria-Palestine that scientific inquiry could begin.

The flurry of archeological work in Palestine in the early decades of this century unearthed a fund of materials inscribed in Hebrew. When combined with inscriptions known from the 19th century, these discoveries made possible a new synthesis of the data. In 1944, W. F. Albright wrote (209):

> It is clear that no *matres lectionis* were written at least in the older poems of the Pentateuch, either in medial or in final position. No special proof is needed for the omission of vowel-letters in medial position, since it is regular in all early Hebrew and all Phoenician inscriptions; in Aramaic documents it was customary until the seventh century B.C. . . .

0 The actual presentation of the synthesis upon which Albright based his conclusion was made by two of his students, F. M. Cross and D. N. Freedman, in their monograph *Early Hebrew Orthography* (hereafter, *EHO*) in 1952.[3] Under the guidance of Albright, they investigated anew the evolution of Hebrew orthography in the biblical period. Working under the assumption that "orthographic patterns followed rigid laws, and like phonetic principles can be classified historically," they evaluated the relevant data, collecting evidence which would shed light on the origin of the use of graphemes to indicate vowels (*EHO*: 59-60). Cross and Freedman concluded that Northwest Semitic orthography was originally purely consonantal and is represented as such in the Proto-Sinaitic inscriptions (Albright 1966), Ugaritic, Phoenician, and 10th-century Hebrew inscriptions (*EHO:* 8-10, 58). During the 11th and 10th

---

[1]The more recent discussions of S. Segert and L. A. Bange are referred to below.

[2]Abraham Ibn Ezra (1089-1164) in *Śāfā B*^{e}*rurah (editio* Lippmann; Fürth, p. 7): "The sages of the Massorah evolved from their inner consciousness reasons why some words are plene and some defective. . . . Behold, the scribe could not do otherwise than write plene when he wanted to preclude the word from being mistaken for its homonym, as for instance ^{c}*wlm*, or defective when he wanted to be shorter." (The citation is from C. D. Ginsburg 1897: 10.)

[3]This was originally submitted as the first half of a joint dissertation at Johns Hopkins University in 1948.

centuries B.C.E., the Arameans, who borrowed the alphabet from the Phoenicians, invented the use of vowel letters to indicate final vowels: *yod* for *ī*, *waw* for *ū*, and *he* for *ā* and *ē* sounds. These final *m.l.* were transmitted to the Hebrews and Moabites, who employed them from the 9th century (*EHO:* 31-32, 58-59).[4] The extension of the use of *m.l.* to indicate medial vowels began in Aramaic during the 8th and 7th centuries and may have spread to Hebrew by the 6th century.

These conclusions have significant implications for the text criticism and interpretation of those parts of the Hebrew Bible which were composed in the pre-Exilic period. Continuing the programmatic work initiated by Albright in "The Oracles of Balaam" (1944), Cross and Freedman applied their results to Judges 5, 2 Sam 1:20-26, Exodus 15, Genesis 49, Deuteronomy 33, and 2 Samuel 22, which they argued were to be dated between the 12th and 8th centuries B.C.E. In the second of their two joint dissertations, *Studies in Ancient Yahwistic Poetry* (1950, published in 1975) each poem was subjected to a "detailed *orthographic analysis*" which involved restoration of the text to the orthography of the period in which it was composed, and then to "a specialized *linguistic analysis*" which involved applying knowledge of the "linguistic structure and vocabulary . . . poetic style and metrical forms" of the Ugaritic texts to these poems (Cross and Freedman 1975: 4-5; emphasis theirs).[5] What was involved specifically in their "linguistic analysis" was more than just an explanation and explication of the biblical text in the light of Ugaritic; it implied restoration of the text according to the more ancient models.[6]

Their method of "linguistic analysis" lies beyond the scope of this study,[7] but their method of "orthographic analysis" is certainly germane. By demonstrating the late origin of *m.l.*, Cross and Freedman implied that their removal from certain texts need not be classified as a conjectural emendation but rather as a scientifically justified restoration of the original. This presupposition is characteristic of many contemporary studies, and its theoretical justification is in need of re-evaluation.[8]

Epigraphic material discovered since the publication of *EHO* has tended to conform to the general pattern of development described by the authors, but not to their timetable.[9] The very year of the book's publication witnessed the successful decipherment of a Hebrew monumental inscription from the end of the 8th century in which the grapheme *waw* was used to indicate the medial

---

[4]Cross and Freedman (*EHO:* 32, 59) admit that historical spellings may have suggested the use of vowel letters to Aramean scribes, but they argue that not enough time elapsed between the borrowing of the alphabet from the Phoenicians and the emergence of a system of writing which consistently represented all final vowels for us to attribute the origin and development of vowel letters exclusively to historical spellings.

[5]Both Freedman and Cross have returned independently to these poems, treating them in ever more sophisticated ways; cf. the "Recent Bibliography," pp. 189-91 in the 1975 reissue. It is particularly important to note that *they have modified their notion of when m.l. were introduced into Hebrew orthography to accommodate new data;* cf. the "Postscriptum" appended to the study, pp. 181-83, and n. 9 below.

[6]The following three passages illustrate such restorations (restored words or letters are enclosed within angled brackets): Judg 5:2, *bhtndb <ndb> ʿm* (p. 13); Judg 5:21, *nḥl qšn grpm / nḥl <qšn> qdmm / qdmm nḥl qšn* (p. 14); Exod 15: 16*b*, *ʿd yʿbr ʿmk yhw / ʿd-yʿbr ʿm<k> z-qnt* (p. 53).

[7]Cf. the critical remarks of D. W. Goodwin 1969: 137-54.

[8]E.g., Dahood 1965-70; Richardson 1971: 257; Christensen 1974: 359-60; Stuart 1976: 25. In his review of Goodwin (1969) M. Dahood dismissed the book's questioning of this and other related presuppositions as irrelevant to modern scholarship, by which, I assume, he means scholarship in the sixties and seventies (1972: 184-85). Cf. also Stuart's remarks (1976: 9) where D. Watson Goodwin is cited as D. W. Watson. Although Goodwin's book analyzes only those papers by Albright, Cross, and Freedman published between 1944 and 1955, it can hardly be considered irrelevant, since work done later employs essentially the same methodology. The primary value of Goodwin's book lies in its criticism of Albright, Cross, and Freedman. The book's weak point lies in its own suggested solutions to the problematic texts which these scholars were trying to treat. (Cf. Cross and Freedman 1972: 413-20. This article, a review of Goodwin's work, faults Goodwin for not reporting on how they have changed their opinions in the light of advances and new discoveries and for offering little in the way of constructive criticism [pp. 417-20].)

[9]Their modified timetable is the following: 1) 11th-10th centuries, completely defective; 2) not later than the 9th century, final *m.l. w, y, h* are "very likely" introduced into Hebrew; 3) no later than the second half of the 8th century, rare instances of medial *m.l. w* and *y*; 4) early 6th century, medial *m.l.* used sporadically (Cross and Freedman 1975: 182).

vowel *ū*.[10] This and subsequent discoveries make a new examination of the corpus of Hebrew epigraphic materials a desideratum.

The basic contention of Cross and Freedman can no longer be maintained, to wit that Northwest Semitic orthography indicated only consonants until vowel letters developed in Aramaic orthography around the 10th century and radiated to Moabite and Hebrew orthography a century later (*EHO:* 8-9, 32-33, 59; 1975: 182).

In Ugaritic, the pronominal suffix of 1s., *ī*, is sometimes indicated by *yod* in the orthography: *aḥdy* (*UT* 51:VII:49), "I, alone," *ḫtny* (*UT* 77:32), "my wedding," *bᶜly* (*UT* 1012:22), "my Lord" (Blau and Loewenstamm 1970: 25-26). The *yod* in *mrym*, *šlyṭ*, *pḫyr*, and in *mym* and *šmym* is most likely a *m.l.* either for a contracted diphthong *ē*, in which case it represents a historical writing, or for the vowel *ī*, in which case it is a pure *m.l.* (Loewenstamm 1969: 111-14; Blau and Loewenstamm 1970: 28-29).[11] The *he* grapheme, at least in the word *ᶜšrh*, which indicates "tens" in numbers between 10 and 20, is a *m.l.* for *ē* (Kutscher 1967: 33-34),[12] while in the vocable *kwt* (RS 20.10,6- unpublished, cited in *UT* glossary no. 1211), the grapheme *waw* may be a *m.l.* for *ū* (Dietrich, Loretz, and Sanmartín 1975b: 560). The second, nonetymological *ʾalep* in *mria* (*UT* 51:VI:41-42; ᶜnt:IV:85), *ṣbia* (*UT* 128:V:19), and *yraun* (*UT* 67:II:6) cannot indicate the glottal stop with its inherent vowel. In each of these words the second *ʾalep* sign must mark a pure vowel, that of the accusative case with the nouns, and of the indicative mood with the verb (*UT* par. 4.5, p. 18; cf. the "normal" spellings, *mra* [*UT* 51:V:107] and *ṣba* [*UT* 125.36]; Loewenstamm 1968: 370; Kutscher 1968: 374; Blau and Loewenstamm 1970: 23-24). *These examples do not comprise a highly developed, consistently applied system of m.l.*, but they do demonstrate that at Ugarit the scribes could and did employ graphemes which usually indicated consonants to indicate vowels.

The Ugaritic data are relevant to the following discussions of 1st-millennium orthography insofar as they demonstrate that an idea of *m.l.* was current in the Canaanite cultural milieu prior to the end of the 2nd millennium. There is not enough evidence to support a definitive statement concerning the influence of this development in Ugaritic cuneiform on the chronologically later linear alphabets. Despite this, the reduced Ugaritic alphabet, approximating the Hebrew-Phoenician phonemic inventory, mirror written from right to left like Hebrew, Phoenician, and Aramaic, may have been a mediating influence. Texts in the reduced alphabet have been discovered at Ugarit itself, at Taanach, Mt. Tabor, Beth Shemesh (*UT:* 16; Dietrich, Loretz, and Sanmartín 1974: 15; 1975a: 548-49), and at Sarepta (Greenstein 1976: 49). Such diverse findspots attest to the wide dissemination of the reduced alphabet in Syria-Palestine. The texts themselves indicate that people speaking dialects akin to Hebrew or Phoenician (*UT:* 16; Greenstein 1976: 57) employed an Ugaritic cuneiform as their alphabet. It may be assumed, though it cannot yet be proven, that the scribes who used the reduced alphabet were also familiar with the manner in which the standard Ugaritic orthography used *m.l.* and were influenced by this usage when they switched to a linear alphabet.[13]

Aramaic inscriptions contemporaneous with the

---

[10]Cf. below, chap. 3, datum no. 29.

[11]Dietrich and Loretz (1967: 541, 547) suggest that *kmyr* (KRT 93) is to be compared with Ugaritic *kmr*, "to pile up" (1Aq 7, 12) and read as a stative **kamir*; *rišyn* (*UT* 173.1; 1106.32) they parse *riš* + *y* + *n* and translate "first month," i.e., *y* = *ī*.

[12]J. Blau, who initially objected to this interpretation (1968b: 267-68), now accepts Kutscher's suggestion (Blau and Loewenstamm 1970: 31).

[13]Although not yet published G. E. Mendenhall's announced decipherment of the Byblos 'hieroglyphics' will certainly contribute to our understanding of this process. Mendenhall remarks that during the Bronze Age, this system had evolved into a syllabary of 30 signs and that it is one of the forerunners of the linear alphabets (1978: 134-35). The significance of these texts to this discussion lies in the hypothesis that the cuneiform Ugaritic alphabet is ultimately modeled after an even earlier linear one and that therefore its Ugaritic orthographic 'irregularities' may be reflections of practices in the earlier system.

An additional wrinkle to any discussion of the prehistory of the Canaanite alphabets and Hebrew orthography is the discovery of a baked clay tablet on which an inscription was impressed with a stylus in what appear to be unknown linear characters. The tablet, from ancient Aphek, derives from the Philistine stratum, although it may be earlier; the signs share many characteristics of both Aegean and early Canaanite systems. (This information was shared with me by Prof. D. Owen in a letter dated 11 May 1979.)

Hebrew inscriptions evaluated below do employ a well-defined, if inconsistently applied, system of *m.l.* The archaic (or archaizing) inscriptions from Zenjirli, which are to be dated between the first and last quarters of the 8th century, 770-730 B.C.E., employ *ʾalep*, *he*, *waw*, and *yod* as *m.l.* in final positions indicating long vowels. *Waw* and *yod* were also employed as *m.l.* to indicate long vowels in medial position which were either naturally long or which had emerged as the result of a contracted diphthong (Kutscher 1972: 50-52; Dion 1974: 55-59, 64-81).[14] In Old Aramaic inscriptions from the 8th century, the same situation prevails,[15] while *yod* as a *m.l.* for a final *ī* is already found in the 10th-9th-century Tel Halaf inscription (*KAI* 231) in the word *zy*. Nothing definitive can be said yet concerning the time and place of the introduction of *m.l.* into Aramaic orthography or the nature of their dissemination. The geographical and chronological dispersion of the data, the troublesome question of local dialect variations in independent political entities, and the paucity of inscriptions preclude such a statement.

Even in Phoenician itself, the bastion of orthographic conservatism, there are sporadic indications that some *m.l.* were employed after the 9th century. The word for "head" is spelled historically with an *ʾalep* in the Kilamuwa inscription from ca. 825 B.C.E., *rʾš* (*rōš*; *KAI* 24.15, 16), where it must be considered a *m.l.* for *ō* (*EHO:* 19). On the 7th-century incantation plaque from Arslan Tash (*KAI* 27.17-18), the final *he* in *šmnh*, "eight," is a *m.l.* for *ā* (Cross and Saley 1970: 45). Here, however, Aramaic practice may have influenced the orthography as it influenced the paleography. The script is typically Aramaic (Cross and Saley 1970: 42). The evidence for *m.l.*, or rather the lack of evidence, permits the statement that no system for representing vowels in the orthography appears to have developed in Phoenician.[16]

Underlying the emergence of any system of *m.l.* is the awareness that graphemes may be assigned more than one value, i.e., that they may be polyphonous. Both the Ugaritic and Phoenician alphabets were originally basically phonemic, each grapheme corresponding to a single consonantal phoneme.[17] Conservative orthographic practices which did not keep pace with certain sound changes gave rise to situations in which graphemes assumed more than one value. In both Ugaritic and Phoenician, scribes employing this insight experimented with using such graphemes as vocalic phonemes in positions where there could be no danger of mistaking them for consonants, e.g., a final vowel. Where historical circumstances did not give rise to enough suitable polyphonous graphemes, scribes could invent new ones, as in the case of the three *ʾalep* signs in Ugaritic, *a*, *i*, *u*, or they could assign a second value to a given grapheme in certain positions within a word. The employment of *ʾalep* signs in Ugaritic and of *he* in Ugaritic and Phoenician as *m.l.* may be due to such an arbitrarily established scribal convention.

What took so long for the scribes of Ugarit and Phoenicia to realize was apparently obvious to the speakers of Greek and Aramaic, who borrowed the Phoenician alphabet. The earliest attested Greek alphabets appear to have been borrowed by the beginning of the 8th century, although the relative uniformity of modifications to the Phoenician system necessitated by the demands of Greek phonology in these suggests an earlier date.[18] The

[14] Dion's suggestion that *m.l.* indicated *short* final vowels (59-62) is problematic; cf. F. Rosenthal's review (1976: 154-55).

[15] Kutscher 1972: 8-11. Kutscher's analysis of *waw* as a *m.l.* for *ū* in medial position is preferable to the overly cautious statements of Degen (1969: 27-28); cf. *EHO:* 31-34. Re. the statements about *ʾalep* as a *m.l.* in the Sefire inscriptions, as well as in those of Bar Hadad, Zakir, or Bar Rakub (*EHO:* 28); cf. the critique of J. J. Koopmans (1962: 7-8) and W. Baumgartner's review of *EHO* (1954: 261), as well as references cited by Degen (1969: 25, n. 4).

[16] This, in contradistinction to Punic, where a highly developed system is attested.

[17] Harris 1936: 11-17; Windfuhr 1970: 50-51. This is implied, rather than stated, by Windfuhr's conclusions.

[18] McCarter 1975: 101-21. McCarter does not discuss the phonological issue, but rather argues that the persistence of certain archaic graphemes, the stance of others, and the different direction of writing necessitate positing a period of experimentation prior to the borrowing of most of the letters (103-21). For a discussion of S. Segert's hypothesis of Aramaic origin, cf. p. 76, n. 71; p. 125, n. 1; and for one of Naveh's suggested dates of borrowing ca. 1100 B.C.E., cf. pp. 113-18.

Naveh's suggestion finds support in the recently published ostracon dating from 1200 B.C.E. (Kochavi 1977: 12). The inscription on the ostracon, written from left to right by an Israelite scribe, attests the early dissemination of writing. For details, cf. Demsky 1977: 14-27. For arguments from Phrygian inscriptions supporting McCarter, cf. West 1978: 347.

most apparent innovation was the employment of the graphemes corresponding to Phoenician ʾ, *h*, *w*, *y*, and ʿ to represent the Greek vowels *a*, *e*, *u*, *i*, and *o* (McCarter 1975: 75). Other innovations, essentially arbitrary, were the use of the grapheme for Phoenician *ḥ* to indicate *ē* (*ēta*) in some scripts, and *h* (*hēta*) in others (McCarter 1975: 95, n. 76), the grapheme for Phoenician *ṭ* to indicate *th*, (McCarter 1975: 95, n. 77), and the invention of a new grapheme to indicate Greek *f* (McCarter 1975: 93-94). These modifications indicate that the Greeks not only borrowed the alphabet but also the idea that it was an arbitrarily developed set of signs which could be adapted to record their significant speech sounds, phonemes.

Aramaic speakers adopted the Phoenician script for recording their language in the 10th century (Naveh 1970b: 14). From the very beginning, Aramaic orthography did not modify the alphabet to accommodate its phonemic inventory; rather, it adopted the principle of polyphony. In Old Aramaic inscriptions, the phonemes *š* and *ṯ* were represented by the grapheme *šin*, *z* and *ḏ* by *zayin*, *q* and *ḍ* by *qop*, and *ṣ* and *ṯ̣* by *ṣade*. In standard Aramaic orthography, after a number of phonemes had coalesced, the scribes changed their orthographic conventions, and phonemes *t* and *t*<*ṯ* were represented by the grapheme *taw*, *d* and *d*<*ḏ* by *dalet*, *ṭ* and *ṭ*<*ṯ̣* by *ṭet*, and ʿ and ʿ<*ḍ* by ʿ*ayin* (Cooke 1903: 185).[19] When this is considered —along with the fact that no known Aramaic inscription follows the early Phoenician practice of representing only consonantal phonemes in the orthography—it must be concluded that Aramaic scribal traditions were innovative and independent. As G. E. Mendenhall has pointed out (1971: 14), the extant evidence indicates that the variety of developments attested in typologically early writing systems is best explained by the anthropological notion of "stimulus diffusion." He explains that a writing system is "stimulated by observation of other cultures, but rarely if ever copied exactly."

Like their Aramean neighbors to the northeast, the Hebrews employed the principle of polyphony when they adopted a Phoenician or Phoenician-type alphabet to their language by the 12th-11th centuries.[20] The grapheme *šin* designated the phonemes *ś* and *š*,[21] and in all likelihood, *ḥet* designated both *ḫ* and *ḥ* and ʿ*ayin* both ʿ and *ġ*.[22]

Whether or not the Gezer calendar of the 10th

[19]Contrast the orthography of *KAI* 214-30 with that of 239-57. The change in orthography can only be explained as arising out of a change in the pronunciation of phonemes *ṯ*, *ḏ*, *ḍ*, and *ṯ̣*. Since the orthographic representation of only these phonemes changed, it is clear that they had not coalesced into *t*, *d*, ʿ, and *ṭ* respectively. (Cf. Ginsberg 1942: 233, n. 24; 1970: 122; Degen 1969: 32-37; Kutscher 1972: 14-19.)

[20]Cf. Kochavi 1977: 3, 12-13, and Demsky 1977: 20-21 for the basis of our dating. The 10th-century date regularly cited for this cultural borrowing was assigned before the discovery of the ʿIzbet Ṣarṭah ostracon, e.g., *EHO:* 43; and Gibson 1971: 1.

[21]Diem argues that the differentiation of the grapheme *šin* into *ś* and *š* took place under Aramaic influence during either a period of Hebrew-Aramaic bilingualism or one in which Aramaic speakers were the traditors of Hebrew linguistic traditions after Hebrew had become a dead language (1974: 243-45). The earliest that this process might have occurred is during the post-Exilic period. Biblical Hebrew, however, contains a number of irregular spellings with *samek* (= *s*) and *śin*, left-dotted *šin* (= *s* < *ś*) in undoubtedly pre-Exilic texts, many of which are most easily explained by presupposing that one of the phonetic realizations of the grapheme *šin* was *s* at the time of the confusion. (Cf. Blau 1970b: 23-24, 114-25, 129 [addendum to p. 23].)

Additonal arguments and a more detailed advocacy of this position can be found in the recent study of Blau (1977, especially pp. 87-88, 100-2).

[22]It is generally believed that *ḫ* > *ḥ* and *ġ* > ʿ early in the 1st millenium B.C.E., but a problem is posed by Greek and Latin transcriptions which show with some inconsistency *χ* for *ḫ*, *γ* for *g*, and zero (ø) for *ḥ* and ʿ.

In 1939, Z. Harris (63) claimed that these different transcriptions ". . . represent merely the attempted transcriptions of the range of actualizations of the [ḥ] and [ʿ] phonemes," while in 1964, S. Moscati (40) suggested that the different forms of transcriptions relate to different periods and do not, therefore, reflect any real phonetic difference.

S. E. Loewenstamm, however, has advanced a solution suggesting that a complex phonetic reality underlies the Greek:

> The transcriptions in the LXX reflect a situation in which ġ/ḫ had already coalesced with ʿ/ḥ, but one in which the earlier stage was remembered . . . Therefore every *χ* / *γ* in the LXX parallels *ḫ*/*ġ* while those with a vowel sign or zero parallel not only *ḥ*/ʿ, but also *ḫ*/*ġ* which had disappeared.

Loewenstamm examined part of the evidence relative to *ḫ* and found that it supports his theory (cited in Blau, 1966: 141).

J. W. Wevers (1970: 110-12) recently examined all of the transcriptions of names and concluded that "it is clear from the hundreds, in fact thousands of instances of *ḥ* by zero or vowel mutation and of *ḫ* by Greek *κ* or *χ* . . that they were still phonemically distinct at the time and place of the old Greek translation, i.e. as late as the second century B.C. " (Among the 211

century B.C.E., the oldest comprehensible Hebrew inscription, contains a *m.l.* remains disputed (Gibson 1971: 1-4).[23] Discussion centers on the status of the final *waw* in *yrḥw*, which occurs four times. Following Albright (1943: 22-24; 1944: 209-11), Cross and Freedman (*EHO:* 57) argue that the *waw* is consonantal, representing a 3 m.s. suffix attached to a dual noun, and is to be pronounced *ēw*, that the orthography of the calendar is completely defective, and that it is representative of Hebrew scribal practices through the 10th century.[24] Other interpretations, however, are possible. It could be taken as an archaic nominative dual construct *ō*,[25] or *aw* (Lemaire 1975b: 17), or as an archaic nominative plural construct *ū* (Garbini 1954-56: 123-30; Gibson 1971: 3).

Each of these suggestions is open to serious criticism which undermines any historical reconstruction of the use of *m.l.* in Hebrew orthography which relies on it. It is therefore discreet to assume with *EHO* that the calendar is Hebrew and that its orthography is defective without, however, opting for one or the other of the problematic solutions.[26] Should later research establish that the *waw* is in fact a *m.l.*, it will be necessary to conclude that the emergence of *m.l.* in Hebrew—if that is indeed the language of the inscription—paralleled chronologically the same development in Aramaic.

On the basis of their assumptions about the Gezer calendar, Cross and Freedman (*EHO:* 57) conclude:

> Since the system of *matres lectionis* was not used in Hebrew before the 9th century, and since that system is substantially the same as the one used in Aramaic from the beginning of that century (if not earlier), and in Moabite from the middle of the 9th century (at the latest), it can hardly be doubted that this system was borrowed by the Israelites from the Arameans during the course of the 9th century B.C.[27]

These conclusions do not necessarily follow from the assumptions made about the Gezer calendar. Among speakers of both Hebrew and Aramaic, the adoption of an orthographic system employing polyphonous graphemes may have given rise independently, or in conjunction with the mediation of the reduced Ugaritic cuneiform, to the notion of *m.l.* This does not deny the possibility or even the likelihood of Aramaic influence on Israelite scribes, but it precludes the necessity of tracing the use of *m.l.* in Hebrew to developments in Aramaic orthography.

In an extensive review of the data available through 1961, L. A. Bange (1971: 140) concludes that *m.l.* first appear at about the beginning of the 6th century B.C.E. as a result of historical spelling. Bange suggests that there were three periods in the linguistic evolution of Northwest Semitic languages and three corresponding stages in their orthog-

---

names examined, Wevers found only 12 exceptions.)

The works of both Loewenstamm and Wevers seem to allow that at least in Judean Hebrew *ḫ* and *ḥ* were phonemically distinct through the pre-Exilic period, but thereafter a process of coalescence began in some dialects. If the same is true of ᶜ and *ġ*, which have not been thoroughly examined, then it is highly likely that the graphemes ᶜ*ayin* and *ḥet* were polyphonous during the pre-Exilic period. (The situation with ᶜ*ayin* is more complex than that of *ḥet*. Cf. Moscati 1964: 38-39, par. 8.45; Bergsträsser 1918: 36-37, par 6d.)

[23]Designation of this inscription as Hebrew is based on historical considerations. It is bereft of any characteristically Hebrew linguistic or paleographic features (Naveh 1968: 69, n. 3; 1970a: 277).

No meaningful text has yet been discovered in the ᶜIzbet Ṣarṭah ostracon beside the abecedary (cf. Demsky 1977: 18-20). Should the meaningless letters eventually yield a comprehensible text, this ostracon might wrest the honor from the Gezer calendar. Naveh, arguing on the basis of paleography, would classify the alphabet as either proto-Canaanite or Canaanite because no distinct Hebrew paleography emerges until the 9th century. Given the site, Naveh suggests that the ostracon might even be Philistine (1978: 33-35). No *m.l.* can be discerned in the ostracon.

[24]Cf. the critique of Albright's position in Goodwin 1969: 35-39.

[25]This was first suggested by H. L. Ginsberg (1935a: 49). The article, unavailable to me, is cited in *EHO:* 46, n. 9. Cf. Albright's criticisms (1943: 22) and those of Gibson (1971: 3).

[26]Cf. the criticism in Gibson 1971: 3 (with qualifications); Goodwin 1969: 35-39; Lemaire 1975b: 16-17. Lemaire's suggestion that the *waw* is an archaic or dialectic dual construct ending assumes that the development of the dual suffix **awim* > *ayim* in the absolute state and **aw* > *ay* > *ē* in the construct state was arrested in the dialect of the inscription in the first stages. His evidence for this is not convincing.

[27]Cf. the summary critique of this argument in Bange 1971: I-II. Bange's study was written in 1961.

raphy. The first period extended from the beginning of the use of consonantal alphabetic script to the 10th century. It was characterized by the use of *yod* and *waw* only as full consonants "if they were followed by a vowel, but by their omission if they were not followed by a vowel, e.g., as diphthongs" (Bange 1971: 139). The second period extended from the end of the 10th to the end of the 7th century in Yaʾudic, Moabite, Aramaic, and Hebrew. It was characterized by what Bange calls "semi-consonantal" orthography, in which *he*, *waw*, and *yod* indicated "off-glides" in accented, long, open syllables while *ʾalep*, the glottal stop, did so in short, accented, open syllables. (Bange holds this last feature to be especially characteristic of the inscriptions from Zenjirli.) During this period, a change in the position of the main stress of words corresponded with the diphthongization of vowels in open accented syllables (Bange 1971: 139). The third period, extending from 600 B.C.E. onward, was characterized by an extension of *he*, *waw*, *yod*, and *ʾalep* to positions where they did not appear in the preceding period and where they could not represent "off-glides." At the beginning of this period, the consonantal element in the diphthongs of the one preceding weakened so that historical spelling gave rise to *m.l.* (Bange 1971: 139-40).

A key concept in Bange's study is that of the "off-glide" element of diphthongs. Diphthongs are complex sounds which change timbre during their emission as a speaker glides from the position of one vowel to that of another in the same syllable (Malmberg 1963: 38). They may be experienced auricularly either as two vowels, e.g., English *house* [au], *fine* [ai], or as a vowel followed by a glide or semivowel, e.g., English *house* [aw], *fine* [ay]. Bange (1971: 2) suggests that in the first linguistic and orthographic period, diphthongs were experienced only as two vowels and were not, therefore, indicated in the orthography which was purely consonantal.[28] In the second period, they were experienced as a vowel followed by a glide, an indefinite sound uttered as the speech organs passed from the articulatory position of the first vowel to that of the second, which was not felt to be vocalic, and was therefore indicated in the orthography. Bange refers to these indefinite sounds as semiconsonants and to their orthographic representation as "off-glides" (1971: 114, no. 6; 119, no. 35; 120, no. 41).[29] He also uses this term to refer to a different phenomenon which will be discussed below. In the last stage diphthongs were contracted into monophthongs, but the orthography of the preceding period was maintained, despite the fact that the off-glides no longer indicated semiconsonants. They came to be viewed as *m.l.* and were then extended to indicate vowels even in positions which had never had diphthongs (Bange 1971: 133-36). The expression "contraction of diphthongs," which is convenient and will be utilized in this study, refers to the phonetic process of vocalic assimilation.[30] In the case of the diphthong [au] or [aw], the low front vowel [a] assimilates to the high back vowel [u], resulting in the mid back vowel [o]; in the case of [ai] or [ay], the low front vowel [a] assimilates to the high front vowel [i], resulting in the mid front vowel [e].

Bange's study is well documented and closely reasoned but is open to criticism at a few significant points which seriously affect his assumptions and preclude an unqualified acceptance of his conclusions.

From the outset, Bange rejects the usefulness of comparative semitics (1971: 2):

> Comparison with cuneiform inscriptions are [*sic*] of no help whatsoever, as they may reflect an earlier or later stage of proto-Semitic. Nor is our knowledge of diphthongs from later Semitic languages of any help, as their diphthongs can be either the product of diphthongization of proto-Semitic monophthongs or the preservation of proto-Semitic diphthongs.

This statement—beside posing the problem of how Akkadian cuneiform reflects an "earlier or later

[28]In general, semitists view these diphthongs as a VC rather than as a VV phenomenon, maintaining that VV > V′V (cf. Moscati 1964: 54-55). Since Bange speaks also of "diphthongization," he may have conceived of this stage as having long vowels in those positions where diphthongs eventually appear, i.e., $\bar{V}$ > VC.

[29]Bange's choice of terminology is not a happy one. The expression *"off-glide"* employs a phonetic term to refer to an orthographic feature, while *"consonant"* is used to refer to the graphemes which indicate consonants as well as to the sounds (e.g., p. 43).

[30]This was brought to my attention by Prof. Sh. Morag, oral communication.

stage of proto-Semitic"—by implication rejects etymological reconstructions which draw upon data from languages which are first attested in later periods, e.g., Arabic. Such languages, however, are necessary to determine whether or not a specific grapheme might or might not reflect a historical consonant. The statement also implies the rejection of information derived from Akkadian transcriptions of Northwest Semitic. The present study has recourse to information derived from both of these sources.

In describing the period of semiconsonantal orthography, Bange posits the existence of a second series of diphthongs whose semiconsonants are represented by off-glides under certain conditions (1971: 42-43, and the following three notes): *āa<a*, indicated by *he* (1971: 47, 72, 102, 131-32); *ūu̯* or *ūw<ū* indicated by *waw* (1971: 49-50, 73, 103, 132); *īi* or *iy<ī*, indicated by *yod* (1971: 51-53, 74, 104, 132). Whereas there is ample evidence of diphthongs formed at two different points of articulation attested in living Semitic languages, and, by learned reconstruction, at earlier stages of these languages, there is little evidence for the second series of diphthongs.[31] In none of the dialects where they are supposed to occur were they ever phonemic or conditioned variants of corresponding monophthongs.

Hebrew epigraphic discoveries and publications since Bange's dissertation was completed in 1961 (e.g., the Arad letters) reveal more inconsistency in the employment of "off-glides" than was apparent in the materials which he studied (1971: 120, nos. 41c, 41d; 121, no. 42). This inconsistency cannot be explained by his notion of "off-glides," which assumes phonetic uniformity with regard to these diphthongs. The notion remains useful in explaining the origin of some final *m.l.* but not in explaining the development of *all m.l.* in *all* Northwest Semitic languages.[32]

In examining epigraphic evidence for the development of *m.l.* in Hebrew orthography, the following criteria are applied: 1) The graphemes *ʾalep, he, waw,* and *yod* are considered *m.l.* if they do not represent etymological consonant phonemes. 2) If, however, they do represent such phonemes, they are considered *m.l.* only when evidence indicates that a sound change occurred and that the grapheme conforms to a historical and not to a phonetic spelling.[33]

The second criterion assumes that the pronunciation of Hebrew in the 9th-6th centuries B.C.E. was different than it is today, and it presumes to know how it was different. The source of this knowledge is historical reconstruction, drawing on comparative Semitic linguistics, based on the text of the Hebrew Bible and on the linguistic traditions associated with it. The function of a reconstruction is to explicate empirical evidence; in itself, it does not constitute such evidence. The reconstruction, however, proceeds from an empirical base and can never surmount the unreliability of this base. For Hebrew the question must be: how reliable are the text and linguistic traditions of the Hebrew Bible as preserved, recorded, and transmitted by the Massoretes, i.e., the Massoretic Text (=MT)?[34]

Discoveries at Qumrân clearly indicate that proto-Massoretic (or proto-*textus receptus*) text types, with regard to contents and orthography, are well represented by the 1st century B.C.E. These existed side by side with texts which differed from them in readings and orthography (Cross 1966: 78-81, 94). Of the three oldest biblical manuscripts, 4QExod[f] (ca. 250 B.C.E.), 4QSam[b] (ca. 225 B.C.E.), and 4QJer[a] (ca. 200 B.C.E.), two, Exod[f] and Jer[a], conform orthographically to the prevailing pattern of the MT (Freedman 1962: 202, 205, 211).[35] The MT, then, may be considered the stemmatic descendant of a text type which evolved prior to the

---

[31]Cf. the critical remarks of Diem 1974: 53-55.

[32]I find this notion most useful in dealing with the orthographic changes between Bange's first and second stages rather than between his second and third stages. The data, however, are sparse. A possible application may be to the study of the synchronic and diachronic distribution of *m.l.* in Ugaritic when and if enough examples are collected.

[33]The limitations of these criteria are discussed in Goodwin 1969: 41.

[34]This term is retained as a useful designation of a type of text rather than as a technical one. For an exposition of this problem, cf. Orlinsky 1966: xxxv-vi.

[35]Anticipating conclusions in the final chapter, this sentence should be qualified to read as follows: ". . . conform orthographically to *what is commonly believed to be* the prevailing pattern of the MT."

3rd century B.C.E., when it is first attested (Goshen-Gottstein 1967: 245-49; Zevit 1977: 327-28). It is not a rabbinic or a massoretic invention, but rather a type of text which was received by them as normative.[36] The antiquity of the text, however, does not assure the antiquity of the linguistic traditions associated with it.

Of the three distinct orthographic elements in the MT, the consonantal text (including graphemes for consonants which quiesced in the course of time), the *m.l.*, and the vowel points, the third was the last to be added to the text. While the first two elements were certainly combined by the 3rd century B.C.E., as evidenced by the proto-Massoretic text types found at Qumrân,[37] the vowel points were not added before the 6th century C.E.[38] The relative lateness of these signs does not indicate that the tradition of pronunciation which they were intended to record and preserve originated in the period of the Massoretes themselves. The text without vowel signs was read orally long before the diacritical marks were invented to indicate vowels. The vowel signs were intended to guide readers in the correct pronunciation of the words according to traditions known to the different schools of Massoretes. As A. Dotan indicates (1971: col. 1409):[39]

> . . . the notes concerning the text of the Bible and the instructions for its proper pronunciation and its exact copying were handed down orally from generation to generation before they were set down in writing. It may be assumed that these comments could be written down and were committed to writing . . . aparently in the sixth or seventh century C.E. Therefore, one must differentiate quite clearly between the oral Masorah which is endless and cannot be defined even though there are allusions to it and evidence thereof, and between the written Masorah whose notations were written in the margins of the codices and which is simply called "the Masorah."

This of course does not imply that the massoretic traditions accurately reflect the manner in which these texts were pronounced by their authors. Nevertheless, the traditions do reflect an archaic phonology. Investigations of Qumranic and Mishnaic Hebrew (ca. 50 B.C.E.-200 C.E.) indicate that postbiblical Hebrew phonology was different than that of biblical Hebrew; e.g., the laryngeals ᵓ and *h* and the pharyngeals ᶜ and *ḥ* became weakened (Kutscher 1974: 505-7; 1971: cols. 1586, 1595-96).[40] Massoretic vocalization indicates that these were not weakened or leveled in the reading tradition, but that they were preserved (Kutscher 1974: 510-11).[41]

As an example of the antiquity of the vocalic traditions preserved by the Massoretes, the case of the 2 m.s. pronominal suffix attached to nouns may be cited. P. Kahle argued that the standard orthography of this suffix with a simple *kap* indicated that it was originally pronounced *ak* and that the pronunciation of *kā* in BH is the result of a massoretic innovation (Kahle 1960: 179).[42] An examination of this suffix in nonbiblical Hebrew texts reveals that the short form predominates

[36]These all-too-brief remarks do not do justice to the complexity of the topic. Cf. the studies collected in the following volumes: M. Goshen-Gottstein, *Text and Language in Bible and Qumran*, 1960; S. Talmon (ed.), *The History of the Bible Text in Recent Writing*, 1968; Sid Z. Leiman (ed.), *The Canon and Masorah of the Hebrew Bible: An Introductory Reader*, 1974; S. Talmon and F. M. Cross (eds.), *Qumran and the History of the Biblical Text*, 1975.

[37]E.g., 4QExod(f): *ᵓwtw (*ᵓoto); ᶜwlm (*ᶜōlām);* 4QJer[a]: *ntwš (*nātōš); ᵓzwr (*ᵓēzōr).* Cf. Freedman 1962: 99-100.

[38]They are not mentioned in the Jerusalem Talmud, which was completed by the first half of the 5th century, in the Babylonian Talmud, which was completed by the end of the 5th century, nor in the earliest Midrashim. However, Asher b. Nehemia (the grandfather of Aaron Ben-Asher) lived, at the latest, in the first half of the 9th century. His grandfather Asher, "the Great Elder," founder of the dynasty of Massoretes, lived in the second half of the 8th century, which means that the vowel signs were fixed before that time (Dotan 1971: cols. 1416-17). On the function of these signs and their early development, cf. Morag 1962: 9-10, 17ff.

[39]Cf. also Goshen-Gottstein 1963: 90-98, especially pp. 94-96. Goshen-Gottstein's study is of particular importance because it exposes the misunderstanding of massoretic activity espoused by P. Kahle which was partially accepted by the authors of *EHO*. For a general appreciation of the massoretic activities and traditions, cf. J. Barr 1968: 194-207; L. L. Grabbe 1977: 179-97.

[40]For Mishnaic Hebrew, cf. the anthology edited by M. Bar-Asher, *Qwbṣ Mᵓmrym Blšwn Ḥzl (Anthology of Articles Concerning Rabbinic Hebrew)*, 1972.

[41]*Pace* Kahle 1960: 169-70. Their retention in Hebrew may have been aided by the fact that they were also distinguished in the Galilean Aramaic spoken by the Tiberian Massoretes (Kutscher 1976: 67-96, especially pp. 89-96).

[42]Despite his discussion of the Dead Sea Scrolls, Kahle's conclusions do not differ appreciably from his earlier treatment of the problem in *The Cairo Geniza*, 1941: 95-102. Cross and Freedman modified Kahle's position, suggesting that *kā* was a form "native to Old Hebrew" which "survived in elevated speech and literary works" (*EHO* 66).

under the influence of Aramaic. Thus, the long form was not preserved in vocalized manuscripts of "literary works," nor was it preserved in the Samaritan reading tradition for the Pentateuch. However, all biblical manuscripts in both the Palestinian and Babylonian systems of vocalization preserve the long form of the suffix (Ben-Hayyim 1954: 51). This indicates that the massoretic vocalization marked a form preserved only in the reading tradition of biblical texts. The common defective orthography of this suffix in the biblical text must then be considered a scribal convention which did not, as a rule, append *m.l.* to the pronominal suffix *kā*.[43]

These, as well as other examples which could be elicited, indicate that the traditions underlying the massoretic vocalization are authentic and archaic, and that when used *critically* they form a reliable base for historical reconstruction.[44]

[43]On *kā* in the DSS, cf. Yalon 1967: 16-18; for *hā*, cf. *EHO* 67; for *hā* and tā, Ben-Hayyim 1954: 39-49, and Yalon 1967: 18-21; and in general, Qimron 1976.

[44]The data collected by A. Sperber (1943) demonstrate the great inconsistency in vocalizations of various forms in the MT. These variations, to the extent that they are not the result of copyist errors, attest to the recording of a living liturgical tradition rather than to the imposition of monolithic phonological principles on the text.

Chapter 2
The Eighth Century—Israel

Beth Shean Ostracon
(9th-8th centuries)[1]

1. *byt?*[ ]: "house/temple of." The *yod* can be interpreted either as a sign that the diphthong was uncontracted in the area of Beth Shean or as a *m.l.* for *ē* in a historical spelling, *byt* for **bēt*.[2]

The Tell-Qasile Ostraca
(early 8th century)[3]

2. *byt:* "house/temple of." The word is written *plene* in *status constructus*. Due to the lack of comparative material in Hebrew, there is no direct proof on which to decide whether this should be read **bayt* or **bēt*.[4] The two spellings *bbth* and *bbyth* in the Mešaᶜ inscription (*KAI* 181.7, 25) indicate that in 9th-century Moabite the diphthong *ay* had contracted to *ē* in unaccented syllables but that the *yod* was sometimes written as a historical spelling. The tendency to maintain traditional orthography is also characteristic of the Hebrew Bible where the spelling *bt* for **bēt* is nowhere attested.[5]

3. *ḥrn:* **ḥōrōn* < **ḥawrōn*,[6] "Horon." This spelling indicates that the diphthong was contracted. The difficulty raised by this ostracon is that

---

[1]The sherd was originally published by N. Tzori (1961: 145-46), who assigned it to the 8th century. J. Naveh, however, dates it to the 9th century (1968: 70, n. 9; 1970a: 278).

[2]Naveh's quasi-suggestion (1970a: 278) that the inscription may be Aramaic is occasioned by the presence of the *m.l.* and not on either paleographical or historical grounds.

[3]Maisler 1950: 265.

[4]This transcription, and those which follow are—and in the present stage of knowledge can only be—approximate reconstructions. Cf. Blau 1970a: 27-38; Gibson 1966: 35-55; and chart 4, "The Phonological Development of Hebrew," compiled by C. Rabin (1971: 67-68). Rabin's chart summarizes the conclusions of Bergsträsser, Birkeland, and Harris. There is some inconsistency in my recording of BH's vocal *šᵉwās* derived from an originally short vowel, and vowels originally short which are long in BH. Sometimes the BH forms have been retained, but most often reconstructed ones are given.

[5]Freedman (1962: 94) writes: "In pre-exilic orthography, the chief evidence for the contraction of the diphthongs is the loss of the original *waw* or *yod*, while the presence of the *waw* or *yod* is evidence of its retention. The situation in post-exilic orthography is complicated by various factors, including the persistence of historical spellings. . . ."

Actually, however, Hebrew orthography furnishes relatively few examples of scribal slips like the Moabite one. In fact, our major proof of the contraction is the massoretic vocalization.

[6]Cross and Freedman write: "*hōrōn* < **hawrān*" (*EHO:* 48). The latter form is difficult to understand since *ā* > *ō* in Canaanite was certainly completed by the end of the Amarna Age. Cf. Harris 1939: 43-44. It is assumed here that this name is connected etymologically to a root *ḥ-w-r*, "cleft, valley between hills," and thus is an accurate description of the city's site, and possibly even that of the south Moabite city Horonaim (cf. Jer 48:5), spelled *ḥwrnn* in the Mešaᶜ inscription (lines 31-32), which has not yet been identified with any degree of certainty. As a geographic name it is similar to Beth Kar (1 Sam 7:11), Beth Hakerem (Jer 6:1), Beth Zur (Josh 15:58), etc. If the *ḥrn* element is theophoric, then the question of the diphthong's contraction may be irrelevant if the

there is no way of knowing whether it represents the pronunciation at Tell-Qasile on the coast or at Beth Horon in the hills of Ephraim (Maisler 1950: 266).[7]

4. *mʾh:* **mēʾā*, "one hundred." The *he* is a *m.l.* for *ā*. The origin of *he* as a *m.l.* is uncertain. It could not have developed out of historical spellings because there are very few cases of consonantal *he* at the end of a word, and these did not quiesce. In the MT they are marked by a *mappīq*. At the beginning or in the middle of a word, *he* is always consonantal. Arguments that *he* was originally consonantal in BH *mā(h)* (i.e., *mah*), and as a directive in words like BH *haᶜi(y)rā(h)* (i.e., *haᶜīrah*), as in Ugaritic, are uncertain. First, its consonantal status in Ugaritic has been challenged (Kutscher 1967: 33-36; Blau and Loewenstamm 1970: 31-32),[8] and second, the internal Hebrew evidence evaluated independently is incapable of yielding a definite solution. This usage may represent an innovation by Hebrew scribes who arbitrarily assigned a vocalic value to *he* in word final position where there was little danger of mistaking it for a consonant. A second possibility is that Hebrew scribes were influenced by the conventions of Aramaic scribes who used *he* for *ā* in word final positions (*EHO:* 24, no. 7 [= *KAI* 202.2]).[9]

5. *ḥyhw:* **ḥiyahū*, a personal name. The *waw* is a *m.l.* for the final long vowel *ū* (Maisler 1950: 266-67).[10] S. Segert (1961: 118) suggests that final long vowels naturally received emphasis, especially in accented syllables, and that a secondary sound *w* or *y* was heard and therefore written, *-ū* > *-ūw* and *-ī* > *īy*.[11]

The Samaria Ostraca (790-770 B.C.E.)[12]

6. *lšmryw* (1:1-2=*KAI* 183): **lašamaryaw*, "to Šamaryaw."[13] The theophoric element *yaw* < *yahu* at the end of a word does not appear to have been contracted (*EHO:* 48).[14] The same is true of the names *ydᶜyw* (1:8=*KAI* 183; **yadaᶜyaw*) and *gdyw* (2:2=*KAI* 184; 6:2-3=*KAI* 185; **gadyaw*).

7. *ywyšḃ* (36:3): **yawyašib* (McCarter 1974: 5) or **yōyašib* (Diringer 1934: 46), a personal name. If this reading of the name is correct—Diringer (1934: 31) considers a reading *yṅ yšṅ*[15]—the name attests to the elision of *he* in the theophoric element even when it occurs at the beginning of names. Akkadian transcriptions of the element

etymology of the divine names is not *II-w*. If so, however, then Moabite *ḥwrnn* could be cited as demonstrating an internal *m.l.* in the 9th century.

[7] The possibility exists, of course, that there was more than one place called Beth Horon.

[8] Cf. The remarks of Blau 1972: 53-54.

[9] Cf. also *znh* (*KAI* 202.14, 18); *DISO:* 18, lines 37-45; 78, lines 38-41; *EHO:* 31.

[10] The closest BH parallel to this name is *ḥī(y)ʾēl* (1 Kgs 16:34). There is no *a priori* reason for this interpretation; but, as Cross and Freedman point out, "the fact that a full system of *m.l.* was employed in the Meša inscription from the middle of the 9th century, suggests strongly that they were being used in Israel at the same time" (*EHO:* 48, n. 20).

[11] Bange (1971: 42-43) refers to this phenomenon as "diphthongization."

[12] For the dates 778-770 and bibliography, cf. *EHO:* 45 and *KAI* II: 183-86. Cross (1962: 34-35), following Yadin, has since argued that the dates should be lowered to the last half of the 8th century primarily on paleographic grounds, but Aharoni (1967a: 322-24; *AI:* 125) convincingly argues against him on both paleographic and historical grounds for dates similar to those which I have suggested. In any event, their 8th-century provenience appears fairly certain. The ostraca are cited according to the standard enumeration as in Diringer 1934; for convenience *KAI* numbers are cited if the ostraca were published there.

[13] The function of the *lamed* is not a point at issue in this discussion, though it is an issue in attempts to interpret the historical significance of the ostraca. The most recent interpretations where relevant literature is cited are by Lemaire (1977: 67-81, especially pp. 71-73) and Shea (1977: 16-17, 26).

[14] The history of the pronunciation of this theophoric element in personal names is extremely difficult to trace for any number of reasons: 1) The data in inscriptions are distributed chronologically over many centuries, linguistically over many languages and dialects, and are represented in many orthographic systems involving unique conventions. Although equations may be established between the representation of the element in one system and its representation in another, phonetic equivalence may not be assumed unless worked out by inner reconstruction from within each system. 2) The significance of the element in Israelite personal names from the biblical period onward may have resulted in socio-linguistic factors complicating the issue even more. Archaic or archaizing pronunciations may have been maintained which diverged from the apparent phonetic realization of a conventionalized orthography, or *vice versa*, an archaic, nonphonetic orthography may have been maintained after sound changes had affected the pronunciation. This is exemplified in the post-Exilic books of Ezra, Nehemiah, and Chronicles.

may indicate that the contraction of the diphthong *aw* > *ō* took place in initial and hence unaccented position.[16] The name *yᶜš* (48:3; **yōᶜaš*) (cf. 1 Chr 7:8; 27:28) also may be cited as indicative of this contraction, but the name is capable of an alternate realization **yaᶜūš* (Diringer 1934: 46; Noth 1928: 196).

8. *ᶜzᵓ* (1:5=*KAI* 183): **ᶜuzzā*, a personal name. Cross and Freedman (*EHO:* 49) suggest reading **ᶜuzzaᵓ* with a consonantal *ᵓalep*. This, however, is uncertain. The form may represent only an Aramaic-type spelling of the name.[17]

9. *ᵓzh* (2:1=*KAI* 184): **ᵓazzā* (?), a place name whose etymology and vocalization are uncertain. The final *he* is most likely a *m.l.* since the number of roots in Hebrew which have a final consonant *he* is very limited (*gbh, kmh, mhh, ngh, tmh*). The same is probably true of the final *he* in *qṣh* (6:2=*KAI* 185), and other similar names mentioned in the ostraca (*EHO:* 49).

10. *yn* (6:3=*KAI* 185; 54:1=*KAI* 187): **yēn*, "wine." The first ostracon indicates that the contraction **yayn* > **yēn* took place in the absolute state of the noun (*nbl yn yšn*, "a jar of old wine"), while the second, that it took place in the construct state (*yn krm htl*, "wine of Kerem Hatel").

11. *šmydᶜ* (Ostraca 29-40, 62-63); *šmdᶜ* (57:2): **šamīdaᶜ*, a clan name (cf. Num 26:32; Josh 17:2; 1 Chr 7:19). The scribal slip into an alternate, defective orthography in Ostracon 57 indicates

---

An examination of the chronological distribution of the suffix in Judean inscriptions indicates that *-yhw* is characteristically pre-Exilic, and *-yh* post-Exilic (cf. the material in Bange 1971: 113-14; Japhet 1968: 338-39). Japhet points out that in Ezra-Nehemiah all names with this element are written *-yh* with one exception, in Ezra 10:41, where an error has entered the text (1968: 339); in Chronicles, however, the *-yhw* form is preferred, even when in the Chronicler's source it may have been written with the short form (cf. Japhet 1968: 339-41 for details). On the basis of the inscriptions, it could be argued that the Chronicler's long form constituted an orthographic archaism not indicative of any phonetic reality in his time. (Cf. the original observation of Ginsberg regarding the diachronic distribution of the theophoric element (1938: 24-25), and the data presented in Coogan 1976: 49-53).

For the contraction of the diphthong in initial positon, see below, n. 16.

[15]Lemaire (1977a: 34) renders it *ywyšᶜ*.

[16]A. Cody (1970: 338-39) has argued on the basis of the spelling of the name Jehoash on the stela of Adad-Nirari III found at Tell Al-Rimah, *Ia-ᵓa-su*, that the diphthong *aw* had already become *ō* in the North in popular pronunciation by the end of the 9th century and that the spelling in the Samaria ostraca may simply be a matter of orthographic conservatism. If Cody's observation that the color of the vowel represented as *a* in the syllable *Ia* was pronounced as [ɔ] is correct, it offers external proof that the shift *aw* > *ō* in unaccented syllables was complete in the North by the beginning of the 8th century.

Malamat (1971: 38-39), proceeding from a different base, points out that since the fuller form of the king's name, Jehoash, would appear in Akkadian as *Ia-u-ᵓa-su*, the extant transcription must represent the actual pronunciation of the name ca. 800 B.C.E.; he suggests that the first sign in Akkadian should be assigned the value *iu* and the name transcribed as *Iu-ᵓa-su*. Malamat thus assumes exactly what Cody set out to prove on the basis of the commonly accepted transcription, *Ia-ᵓa-su*, namely that the *he* was syncopated and the resulting diphthong contracted. (Regarding the elision of *h*, even earlier in the 9th century, cf. McCarter 1974: 5). The basis for his assumption is the use of the short form in the biblical text, but there it may be an anachronism since the composition of the sections about Joash/Jehoash were not set down in his lifetime. The short form could then represent a later form of his name (cf. Cody 1970: 325, n. 1). Malamat does not discuss the problems inherent in taking the biblical forms at face value.

S. Norin (1979: 97) advances a thesis which appears to support Malamat's assumption and to complement the conclusions of S. Japhet described above in n. 14: The theophoric element used at the beginning of names was *yw-* in pre-Exilic times and *yhw-* in post-Exilic times. Unfortunately, the thesis remains unproven.

The extrabiblical materials, ostraca, stamps, and seals, which Norin presents do not support his contention (1979: 88-89). Three of his nine major data are undated (and one of these is from Carthage), two are dated between 600-300 B.C.E., and one is dated to either the pre-Exilic period or the Roman period (1979: 88). In order to explain so-called post-Exilic forms in pre-Exilic texts, and *vice-versa*, he has recourse to arguments based on the theology of the Deuteronomistic writers/editors who changed *yw-* names to *yhw-* ones to give them a more religious sound (1979: 94-97). The theological explanation is a contribution to the study of biblical literature; his thesis concerning the diachronic distribution of the *yw/yhw* element, however, remains undemonstrated.

In any event, his reconstruction of the prefixed element *yw* coincides with the one proposed above in that it assumes an original element with *he, yhw*, which is chronologically prior to it (1979: 93).

Of significance for this discussion is the fact that Cody, Malamat, and McCarter agree that the cuneiform evidence indicates that the *he* was elided. The recently published *lywᵓr* seal from the end of the 8th or beginning of the 7th century might be relevant to this discussion could its provenance be established. In it, the *he* of the theophoric element is syncopated: **yōᵓō/ūr* or **yawᵓō/ūr* < **yahūᵓō/ūr* (Avigad 1969: 6-7).

[17]In BH, the same name is spelled *ᶜzh* in pre-Exilic 2 Sam 6:6-8 but *ᶜzᵓ* in the parallel text in post-Exilic 1 Chr 13:7-10. This

that the *y* which is commonly employed in the writing of this name is a *m.l.* for *ī* (Bange 1971: 116-17). This is an anomaly, since the vowel is not indicated in any of the other names in which it occurs, e.g., *ᵓbbᶜl* (2:4=*KAI* 184; **ᵓabībaᶜal*), *ᵓḥnᶜm* (19:4=*KAI* 186; **ᵓaḥīnōᶜam*), etc.

12. *ymnh* (Diringer 1934: 71): *yimnē* or *yimnε̄*, "he shall count." The final *he* is a *m.l.* for *ē* or ε̄.[18]

The following five data of southern provenience are introduced in this chapter to enable a convenient contrast and comparison between them and those from northern epigraphs. They will also be considered in the discussions of the following chapter.

A Seal from the Area of Lachish (middle or late 8th century)[19]

13. *ḥnh*: **ḥannā*, a woman's name (cf. 1 Sam 1:2). The *he* is a final *m.l.* for *ā*.

An Inscribed Bowl From North Sinai (8th century)[20]

14. *ᶜbdyw*: **ᶜōbadyaw*, a man's name. As in the Samarian ostracon from the north where the same name is attested (Ostracon 50:2), there is no evidence for the contraction of the diphthong in the theophoric element at the end of the name.

15. *ᶜdnh*: **adnā*, a man's name (cf. 2 Chr 17:14). The final *he* is a *m.l.* for *ā*.

16. *yhw*: **yahū*, the name of the deity. The final *waw* is a *m.l.* for *ū*.[21]

The Jotham Seal from Elath (8th century)[22]

17. *ytm*: **yōtām*, "Jotham." The orthography indicates that the following phonetic developments had taken place in the theophoric element under as of yet unspecified conditions: *yahū* > *yaw* > *yō*.

Summary and Conclusions: Orthography of the 8th Century

The data analyzed in the preceding section derive from two politically and geographically distinct areas, Israel and Judah; conclusions based on them must take this into account.

The Tell-Qasile ostraca demonstrate the use of *waw* to indicate a final, long *ū* (no. 5), and of *he* to indicate a final *ā* (no. 4). The defective spelling *ḥrn*

---

ostracon would indicate that the name was already spelled with both a *he* and an *ᵓalep* in pre-Exilic Israel and suggests that both were pronounced the same way, i.e., **ᶜuzzā*.

[18]Other readings of this ostracon, C-1101, are possible. Cf. Diringer 1934: 72; the discussion of Birnbaum in Crowfoot, Crowfoot, and Kenyon 1957: 11-12; Lemaire 1977a: 246-48.

There is a question whether or not the ε phone may be posited for pre-Exilic Hebrew. Although clearly represented by a *sĕgōl* in the Tiberian system of vocalization, it is represented neither in the Babylonian one, which has one sign for Tiberian *pataḥ* (= *a*) and *sĕgōl*, nor in the Sephardic tradition of pronunciation, which fails to distinguish between a Tiberian *ṣērê* and *sĕgōl*—but does mark the distinction between *pataḥ* and *sĕgōl* (Ben-Hayyim 1978: 95-96).

Whereas these data could be interpreted to indicate that the ε is coalescing in the traditions where it is not clearly marked and is therefore an ancient feature, Ben-Hayyim argues, on the basis of these data and data derived from the Samaritan reading tradition of the Torah, that the emergence of ε as a distinct phone is late and was perceived as unique only by the Tiberian massoretes who marked it (1978: 100-1). In addition, against the prevailing view that considers ε an allophone of both *ē* < *i* and *a*, he argues that it is only an allophone of *a*, and that where ε appears to be derived from *i*, *i* > *a*, a fact which can be verified in the Samaritan tradition which still preserves the *a* (1978: 101-3).

Although Ben-Hayyim has advanced the discussion of this problem in Hebrew phonology, his arguments are insufficient to explicate all of the data bearing on the problem, and this forces him into extremely complicated hypotheses with which he himself does not appear too content (1978: 101-4).

We have chosen to indicate ε or ε̄ in our reconstructions, usually as allophones of *ē*, suggesting that these may have been ancient allophones which only the sophisticated Tiberian system preserved. In no case, however, does this affect our arguments concerning *m.l.*

[19]Bartlett 1976: 59-61.

[20]Meshel and Meyers 1976: 8. The site of the find is an 8th-century Judean fortification excavated by Meshel at Kuntillat ᶜAjrud in northeast Sinai.

[21]The complete text reads as follows: *lᶜbdyw bn ᶜdnh brk hᵓ lyhw*, "For Abadyaw son of Adna. He is blessed to Yahu." Note the differences between the theophoric element in the personal name and the divine name itself.

[22]Glueck 1940: 13-15; Avigad 1961: 18-19. For the date cf. p. 19. For a discussion concerning the Judean ethnicity of the occupants of Stratum 3, cf. Meshel 1975: 53.

attests to the contraction *aw* > *ō* under certain phonetic conditions (no. 3).[23] In the Samaria ostraca, both ᵓ*alep* and *he* are used as *m.l.* for a final *ā* (nos. 8, 9) while *he* is also used to indicate a final *ē* or *ɛ̄*. From the orthography of names containing the theophoric element *yaw*, it is clear that under certain phonetic conditions, the *he* was elided, i.e., *yahū* > *yaw* (no. 6);[24] and from the spelling of the word *yn*, that the contraction *ay* > *ē* had occurred (no. 10).

If these data are said to be representative of the northern dialect of Hebrew, then the following observations are in order: 1) the contraction of the diphthong *aw* > *ō* took place in unaccented syllables but not in accented ones; 2) the contraction of the diphthong *ay* > *ē* took place in both accented and unaccented syllables. Therefore, the orthography of the name *ywyšb* (no. 7) must be historical with *waw* functioning as a *m.l.* for *ō*;[25] the spelling *byt* (nos. 1, 2) must also be historical and the *yod* considered a *m.l.*, since the word was pronounced **bēt*.[26] Finally, *yod* was also used as an internal *m.l.* for the vowel *ī* in the name *šmydᶜ* (no. 11).

The data of southern provenience demonstrate that *he* was used to indicate the final vowel *ā* (nos. 13, 15), while *waw* was used to indicate the final vowel *ū* (no. 16). The orthography of the Jotham seal appears to indicate that in the south, as in the north, *he* was elided in the theophoric element of proper names and that the resulting diphthong was contracted in unaccented syllables (no. 17).

---

[23]The intermediary stage of the process **ḥawrā́n* > **ḥawrṓn* > **ḥōrṓn* is partially represented in the orthography of *ḥwrnn* (Mešaᶜ = *KAI* 181.31, 32).

[24]Cf. the discussion in n. 14 (chap. 2).

[25]Note the orthography of the name *ḥwrṣ* on a Hebrew seal of unknown provenience dated by Herr (1978: 122) on paleographic grounds to the late 8th century. The pattern of the name is that of a *Qal* participle, and the *waw* is clearly a *m.l.* The seal, however, could have originated in the 7th century B.C.E. (Cf. Herr 1978:4 for an explanation of "typological" dating in "chronological" terms.)

[26]Cross and Freedman (*EHO:* 57) consider these sites characteristic of the North Israel dialect of Hebrew and admit that *byt* is an anomalous form. Rather than draw the conclusion which I have drawn about the orthography, they conclude that the abnormality lay in the pronunciation of the word with an uncontracted diphthong and that this was the result of dialectal mixture (*EHO:* 48). It must be noted that by admitting the presence of different local dialectal treatments of the diphthong, they effectively disqualify this contraction as a characteristic of North Israelite Hebrew.

Chapter 3
The Eighth-Seventh Centuries—Judah

A Hebrew Graffito (8th-7th centuries)[1]

18. *ʾrr:* **ʾārūr*, "cursed <be>." The vowels are not indicated by *m.l.*.

19. *ymḥh:* **yimḥē* or **yimḥɛ̄*, "efface." The final *he* is a *m.l.* for *ē* or *ɛ̄*.

20. *brk:* **bārūk*, "blessed <be>."[2] The vowels are not indicated by *m.l.*

Wine Jar Inscription (8th century)[3]

21. *yyn kḥl:* **yayin kōḥel*, "wine of Kōhel" (Avigad 1972: 4-5). The orthography of *yyn* does not indicate whether or not the diphthong *ay* remained uncontracted in unaccented syllables (cf. no. 9; no. 30, below).

A Hebrew Seal (8th-7th centuries)[4]

22. *lhwšʿ:* **lahawšēaʿ* or **lahōšēaʿ*, "of Hoshea." Which of these two possible phonetic realizations is most probable depends on the nature of the medial *waw*, which will be discussed in the summary below.

The Third Tomb Inscription from Khirbet el-Kôm (8th-7th centuries)[5]

23. *ktbh* (line 1): **katabō*, "his inscription" (Dever 1970: 159; Lemaire 1977b: 600-1). The final *he* is a *m.l.* for the 3 m.s. pronominal suffix, *ō*. These and other similar suffixes could not have been pronounced *hū* since the final vowel would then have been indicated by a *waw* (cf. data nos. 44, 54).

24. *brk* (line 2): **bārūk*, "blessed <be>." The vowels are not indicated by *m.l.*

25. *yhwh* (line 2): **yahwē* or **yahwɛ̄*, "Yahweh." The final *he* is most likely a *m.l.* for *ē* or *ɛ̄*.

26. *ʾšrth* (line 3): **ʾšēratō*, "his Asherah." The *he* is a *m.l.* for the 3 m.s. pronominal suffix *ō*. Cf. on the same line *lh*, **lō*, "(to) him."[6]

---

[1] Bar-Adon 1975: 226-32. For the date, cf. p. 231. The graffito was found in a cave overlooking the Dead Sea.

[2] Perhaps this is to be rendered as an imperative (Bar-Adon 1975: 229).

[3] Avigad 1972: 2-5. The jar originated in the Hebron area.

[4] Driver 1955: 183. The seal, of unknown provenience, is in the Ashmolean Museum at Oxford. Driver considered it pre-Exilic.

[5] Dever 1970: 159. This inscription, no. 3, is dated paleographically by the author to the middle of the 8th century (162-65). Lemaire also suggests a date ca. 750 (1977b: 602-3), but Dever reports that Cross prefers a date ca. 700 (165).

[6] For this reading, cf. Lemaire 1977b: 599-600. The *he* cannot be taken as a defectively written suffix *-ahū*, because the final vowel *ū* is represented by a *waw* in this inscription in the name *ʾryhw*. For *ʾšrth* with the same sense and in the same context at Kuntillet ʿAjrud, cf. Meshel 1978: opposite fig. 10.

Lemaire (1977b: 599) reads the beginning of line 3 *mṣryh*, "by his enemies." This improves upon Dever's original tentative reading *mʾrr* (1970: 159) but is still beleaguered by difficulties. Before Lemaire's *reš* there is the tail of another letter, perhaps a *reš*,

26.[bis] *hwš*ᶜ (line 3): **hawšaᶜ* or **hōšaᶜ*, "help." (Cf. datum no. 22.)

The Silwan Inscription
(8th-7th centuries)[7]

27. *zᵓt* (lines 1, 3): **zōt*, BH *zō(ᵓ)t*, "this." The *ᵓalep* is not etymological and must be considered a *m.l.* for *ō* (Tsevat 1960: 83-84).[8] The form already appears in Moabite in the middle of the 9th century (*KAI* 181.3).

28. *ᵓmth* (line 2): **ᵓamatō*, "his concubine." The final *he* is a *m.l.* for the suffixed pronoun *ō*. Cf. also *ᵓth* (line 2), "with him," **ittō*.

29. *ᵓrwr* (line 2): **ᵓārūr*, "cursed." The medial *waw* is a *m.l.* for *ū*.

Arad Ostraca
(701 B.C.E.)[9]

AI 40[10]

30. *bnkm* (line 1): The interpretation of the form is problematic. It could be read **binkim* (*AI*: 72), "your (pl.) son (sing.)," but this reading must confront the following objection: since the letter is addressed to a single individual, Malkiyahu, by two people, Gemar[yahu] and Neḥemyahu, the form of the noun should have been *bnk* or *bnyk*, BH *bānɛ(y)ka*, "your (sing.) sons (pl.)." Aharoni (1970: 30-31) suggests that the plural suffix is employed because Malkiyahu represented the authorities to whom the senders were responsible.

---

and after his *reš* there is still another *reš*. The semivertical sign which he has indicated as a word divider is connected to three (and perhaps four) visible semihorizontal lines and could be an additional *he*. However, assuming that his reading is correct, *ṣryh* (**ṣārayō*) reveals the uncontracted diphthong in the nominal plural before a 3 m.s. pronominal suffix and is a significant link in reconstructing the history of this and related forms. Cf. below data nos. 30, 72, 75, and especially 99 with their accompanying notes.

[7]Avigad 1953: 137-52; *KAI* 191. If the tomb is associated with Shebna mentioned in Isa 22:15, 16, then the inscription should definitely be dated to the last part of the 8th century.

[8]In BH, an archaic demonstrative pronoun *zō(h)* appears about 15 times, thrice in the expression *kāzō(h) wᵉkāzɛ(h)* (Judg 18:4; 2 Sam 11:25; 1 Kgs 14:5) and elsewhere independently, e.g., Josh 2:17; 2 Kgs 6:19; etc. This would appear to be the original form before secondary feminization took place and *zō* > *zōt*. The longer form *zōt* could not be spelled with *he* as a *m.l.* in the middle of the word, so *ᵓalep* was employed on the model of *rᵓš (rōš)*, and *ṣᵓn (ṣōn)*, where it remained as a historical spelling (cf. Sherman 1966: 24, n. 42).

In a 5th-4th-century Phoenician inscription from Byblos, the feminine demonstrative adjective is spelled three times *zᵓ* (*KAI* 10.6, 12, 14). The spelling is also found on a broken 9th-century inscription from Cyprus, where it appears to be a masculine form: *qbr zᵓ* (*KAI* 30.2).

Avigad (1970: 290-91) suggests that *ᵓalep* may also appear as a *m.l.* on a Moabite seal of the 8th-7th century: *lkmš mᵓš*, "< Belonging > to Kemosh, the Lord." *mᵓš* is taken as the *plene* spelling of a theophoric element spelled defectively in Ugaritic, *mṯ*, and in Biblical Hebrew *mš*. The etymology and meaning of the word, however, are still uncertain, and Avigad's suggestion can only be considered tentative. Cf. Rocco 1970: 396, 399; Bordreuil 1975: 113.

[9]The dates adopted in this study for the Arad ostraca are those suggested by Y. Aharoni, the excavator of Arad and the publisher of the ostraca (1970: 18, 28-29, 33-34; *AI*: 1-8). Although originating in the last decade of the 8th century, the Arad ostraca cited below are included here because they are of southern origin, as are most of the Hebrew epigraphic remains of this century, and can be considered representative of the orthography at the beginning of the 7th century.

Since the dates of the ostraca are assigned on the basis of the dating of the archeological context in which they were found—and not purely on that of paleographical charts compiled before their discovery and developed from inscriptions at other sites—it should be noted that Aharoni's archeological dating of Arad, and his concomitant dating of other sites such as Lachish and Beer-Sheba, have not gone unchallenged.

Yadin (1965: 180) and Nylander (1967: 56-59) both challenged that tool marks on the casemate wall of Stratum 7, dated by Aharoni to the 7th century B.C.E., were made by a tool invented only in the middle of the 6th century. An examination of Assyrian reliefs in the British Museum, however, indicated that the tool in question, a claw-chisel, was already in use in Assyria by the 8th century, and hence its appearance in Judah in the 7th century should occasion no surprise (Aharoni 1967c: 89-90). Cf. also Yadin 1976: 5-6, and nn. 1, 2, 3, 14; a counter argument by Rainey, cited by Freedman (1976: 7); the remarks of Oren concerning Tell esh- Sheriyeh, also cited by Freedman (1976: 7-8); and those of Freedman himself on the hope that D. Ussishkin's work at Lachish might resolve the issue (1976: 8); Ussishkin 1977: 53; 1978: 93; M. and Y. Aharoni 1977: 53; Herzog *et al.* 1977: 49-58; and M. Aharoni 1977: 67-68. If these challenges are correct, a reassignment of dates to the strata at Arad as well as to the ostraca would be necessary. The implications of new dating would place the ostraca dealt with in items 30-35 in the middle rather than at the beginning of the 7th century. Nevertheless, although the debate on this and related issues has been sharp and protracted, the preponderance of evidence still appears to favor Aharoni's evaluation of the matter (cf. also n. 34, below, concerning the stamped Judean jar handles).

[10]The numbering of the Arad ostraca follows that of Aharoni in *AI*.

This, however, fails to account for the singular form of the noun.[11] Since the plural form is demanded by the context, a form *bnykm* with a *yod* might have been expected; in the absence of the *yod*, it may be assumed that the diphthong *ay* had contracted in unaccented syllables: **banaykim* > *banēkím*.[12]

31. *hʾyš* (line 7; cf. line 8): **haʾīš*, "the man." It is generally assumed that this common word is derived from a root *ʾwš* or *ʾyš*, but the existence of such a root is moot, and there are no clear parallels in cognate languages.[13] From the vocalization of this word in the MT, it is quite clear that the vowel is *ī*, and there is no indication that the *yod* by which the vowel is consistently represented was ever consonantal; the *yod* must therefore be considered a *m.l.* for a medial vowel *ī* (cf. below, no. 40.).

32. *ydʿth* (line 9): **yadaʿtā*, "you knew." If the *he* actually ends this word and is not the first consonant of the following one (which is lost because the ostracon is broken), it is a *m.l.* for a final *ā* (or *a* [?]).

33. *rʿh* (line 15): **rāʿā*, "evil." The *he* is a *m.l.* for final *ā*.

AI 50

34. *mrmwt:* a personal name. In BH, *mᵉrēmō(w)t* (Ezra 8:33; 10:36; Neh 3:4, 21—all spelled *plene* with a *waw*). The medial *waw* will be discussed in the summary below.

An Ostracon From Beer-Sheba (701 B.C.E.)[14]

35. *mn tld* (line 2): **min tōlad*, "from Tolad." This place name, on a receipt, is to be identified with BH *(ʾel) tō(w)lad*, mentioned in Josh 15:29; 19:4, and *tō(w)lād*, mentioned in 1 Chr 4:29, a city in the Negev (Aharoni 1973: 71). In BH, the name is spelled *plene*, employing an etymological *waw* as a *m.l.* in a historical spelling. The defective spelling on this ostracon indicates that the *waw* was no longer heard, i.e., **tawlád* > *tōlád*.

The Siloam Tunnel Inscription (ca. 700 B.C.E.)[15]

36. *wzh* (*KAI* 189.1): **zē* or **zε̄*, BH *zε̄(h)*, "this." The final *he* is a *m.l.* for *ē or ε̄*.

37. *hyh* (line 1): **hayā*, BH *hāyā(h)*, "was." The final *he* is a *m.l.* for *ā*. It also occurs in *brkh* (line 5), "pool," BH *bᵉrēkā(h)* and *ʾmh* (lines 5-6), BH *ʾammā(h)*, "cubit."

38. *hnqbh* (lines 1, 3-4): While the exact translation of this word is still a subject of debate, the status of the final *he* as a *m.l.* is certain. It may be a *m.l.* for *ō* if the word is to be vocalized as a verbal noun **hinnaqibō*, "its being tunneled through" (*EHO:* 49),[16] or if it is to be vocalized as a regular noun **naqūbā, *naqībā* or the like, "tunnel," the *he* is a *m.l.* for *ā*.

39. *bʿwd* (lines 1, 2): "while yet." Cross and Freedman (*EHO:* 50) read this **baʿawd*. The medial *waw* will be discussed in the summary below.

40. *ʾš* (lines 2, 4): BH *ʾī(y)š*, "man, each one."

41. *rʿw* (lines 2, 3, 4): "his fellow." In BH *rēʿō(w)*, once (Jer 6:21), as opposed to more than 115 occurrences of *rēʿēhū(w)*, a regular suffixed form of **rēʿε̄* < **rēʿayi*. The pronominal suffix

---

[11] Aharoni (1970: 30-31) interprets *bnkm* "your (pl.) son(sg.)" in contrast to his Hebrew vocalization *binᵉkem*, given first in 1969b: 15 and repeated in *AI:* 72. He does not discuss the implications of his Hebrew vocalization or English translation.

[12] It is not certain that two men sent this letter: the name Gemaryahu is restored; the conjunction *waw* before Nehemyahu is partially erased; the *mem* of *šlḥ[m]*, "are sending," indicating a plural participle, in line 2 is likewise restored, while verbal and nominal suffixes elsewhere in the letter are 1st singular (lines 3, 6, 10). Therefore, although Aharoni's interpretation is probable, it is not certain, and the above reconstruction of the phonology, based on Aharoni's understanding of the text, must likewise be considered probable but not certain.

[13] Cf. *KB, BDB, ad ʾyš*; and *DISO ad ʾšı* where the panoply of *plene* and defective spellings in the various Northwest Semitic dialects is revealed. Possibly, there may be an etymological connection between *ʾi(y)š*, "man," and the particle expressing existence, *ʾiš/yēš*, = Ug. *i̱t* = Phoen. *ʾš* (Gevirtz 1957: 125). For a summary of current uncertainties, cf. Bratsiotis 1974: 222.

[14] Aharoni 1973: 71. For a discussion of the problems of this dating, cf. above n. 9.

[15] *KAI*: II, 189. G. Levi Della Vida (1968: 164) has pointed out that the nature of the inscription is such that it may have been a copy of a literary narrative or chronicle. If this be so, its orthography is extremely important, since it would reflect an official orthography used in Jerusalem circles.

[16] Moscati already questioned this interpretation in his review (1954: 135).

ēhū with singular nouns is generally restricted to those whose third root consonant was originally *yod* (Barth 1913: 49, par. 19b; Blau 1976: 25, par. 7.2.1.5.2). The form in this inscription and in Jeremiah may be explained as a new singular derived by backformation from a regular plural **rē^{c}īm* > **rē^{ac}*, which was no longer felt to be a *III-y* noun (*GKC:* §84^{a}i). The form **rē^{ac}* fell into the *qēl* class of nouns, with words such as *^{c}ēṣ, ^{c}ēd* (< *^{c}wd), lē^{a}ḥ* (< *lḥḥ*), and *dē^{ac}* (< *yd^c*), and therefore used the more common pronominal suffix applied to these nouns, *ō*.[17]

42. *ql* (line 2): "voice." Cross and Freedman (*EHO:* 50; cf. 24) vocalize this **qāl*, arguing that it is not to be related to **qawl* > *qōl* but to Biblical Aramaic *qāl*, Syriac *qālâ*, Ethiopic *qal*, etc. The Hebrew evidence is equivocal regarding the etymological derivation of the word.[18] Judging, however, from the vocalization of the word in the MT, it should be vocalized **qōl*. If, as they maintain, it is to be associated with an original **qāl*, then this would have become **qōl* by the well known *ā̆* > *ō̆* shift which took place by the Amarna Age (Harris 1939: 43). If, on the other hand, it is to be associated with an original **qawl*, then the orthography would indicate that the word is spelled defectively and that the change *aw* > *ō* had taken place in southern Hebrew in unaccented syllables: *ql $^\supset$š*, "the voice of a man."

43. *wbym* (line 3): "and on the day." Cross and Freedman (*EHO:* 24, 50, 53) vocalize this **wabayām*, arguing that there existed in Hebrew a series *ym/ymt*, parallel to *ywm/ywmt* as in ESA. This case seems similar to that of *ql* above, except that unlike *ql* there is reason to infer from the regular BH plural *yāmīm*, originally **yamīm*, that at one time a biradical singular **yam* may have existed in Hebrew or in proto-Hebrew.[19] However,

---

[17]Cross and Freedman (*EHO:* 50) suggest that the word, both here and in Jeremiah should be read **rē^{c}ēw* < **rē^{c}ēhū* (with syncope of the *he*). This explanation poses two difficulties. First, as a rule, in Hebrew *h* in the pronominal suffix was preserved after long vowels (cf. Blau 1976: 25, par. 7.2.1.5.1). Second, it is difficult to reconcile this with the fact that they consider the final *he* in *hnqbh* to be a *m.l.* for the 3 m.s. pronoun *ō* (*EHO:* 49-50). The spelling with *h* presumably originated when the pronoun suffix was still pronounced *-ahū* and the development *-áhū* > *áw* > *ō̆* had not yet taken place (cf. *EHO:* 54). The pronunciation *ō* elsewhere indicates not only that the syncope of the *he* was an event of the past but also that the pronunciation which Cross and Freedman posit here could not have been a current development in common speech resulting from a recent change, i.e., syncope of *he*. Their difficulties arise from the assumption that *r^{c}w* must be derived from *rē^{c}ēhū(w)* and that *waw* could not possibly be a *m.l.* for *ō* (even in Jeremiah?). In addition, the hypothetical diphthong *êw* which they posit is left without a history. Was it ever contracted? (In Greek, ε̄ +ω=ω, i.e., *ew* > *ō*, but there is no evidence for a corresponding development in Hebrew.) When and why did it fall out of use? It is simpler to assume that the *waw* is used here as a *m.l.* for *ō*.

In more recent discussions of this suffix, Freedman (1962: 93) writes: ". . . in pre-exilic inscriptions the 3rd masculine singular suffix attached to nouns in the singular is regularly represented by the letter *he*, whereas in the documents [from Qumran], as in MT commonly, *waw* is used. The vowel in question was presumably *ô*, though this is not certain for pre-Massoretic vocalization (i.e. we are dependent upon Massoretic vocalization for this pronunciation: it may have been *uh* in pre-exilic times and possibly *aw* later, contracted to *ô* in post-exilic times."

Cross (1970: 305, n. 3) writes: "It has become increasingly clear that the Judean 3 masc. sing. pronominal suffix was originally *-ū* > - *ō* (derived from *-uhu*). . . ."

Freedman's statement is somewhat noncommital and vague, "may . . . possibly." There is, however, no phonetic explanation for the development *uh* > *aw* > *ō* which he posits. Gordis (1937: 92-94) lists 52 examples of the suffix rendered by a *he* in the *k^{e}tîb* of the MT; cf. Ginsburg 1897-1905: vol. IV, 286-87.

Cross' statement is quite definite but highly doubtful. If the sound change *ū* > *ō* took place, it should have taken place wherever *-ū* appeared, in the perfect and imperfect of verbs, e.g., *šām^{e}rū, yišm^{e}rū*; in the 3 m.s. pronoun *hū, hū($^\supset$)*; and in certain nouns such as *$^\supset$āḥū*.

[18]The word is often spelled without a *m.l.* in MT, a fact which could be interpreted as representing the pristine spellings: e.g., Exod 3:18; 4:8, 9; 5:2; 9:23, 28, 29, 34; 19:16; 23:21, 22.

[19]The original shortness of the vowel is revealed in forms such as *y^{e}mē(y)*.

For the form **yām*, Cross and Freedman cited Ginsberg 1935: 79. Ginsberg, however, argued that the word should read *yam*, with a short vowel, and cited Noeldeke. Noeldeke (1910: 133), arguing on the basis of comparative evidence primarily from Hebrew, Aramaic, Syriac, and Arabic, concluded that the word for "day" was originally a biradical substantive from which other forms developed. He nevertheless believed that in the Shiloah inscription and in the Moabite Stone, it was to be pronounced **yōm* (134, n. 1). J. Barth (1906: 790-91), who accepted Noeldeke's argument, pointed out that the plural *yāmīm* cannot be derived from the biradical singular **yam* which either existed alongside *yawm* or out of which *yawm* developed in proto-Semitic. The plural of **yam* should have been **yammīm*, which does not occur. Barth maintained, then, that the extant plural *yāmīm* was formed by analogy to *šānīm*.

the consistent *plene* spelling *ywm* in the MT apparently indicates that a second singular, **yawm* can be posited.[20] *If* this is the word in the inscription, the defective spelling indicates that in southern Hebrew *aw* > *ō* in unaccented syllables: *ym hnqbh*, "the day of the tunnel."[21]

44. *hkw* (line 4): **hikkū*, "they struck." The final *waw* is a *m.l.* for *ū*. Cf. also, *wylkw* (line 4), "and they flowed."

45. *hmym* (line 5): **hammaym*, "the water." The diphthong *ay* has not been contracted here or in *mʾtym* (line 5), **maʾtaym*, "two hundred" (*EHO:* 51).

46. *mwṣʾ* (line 5): "the source." Cross and Freedman (*EHO:* 51) vocalize this **mawṣaʾ*. The medial *waw* will be discussed in the summary below. Whether or not the final *ʾalep* had quiesced by this time is difficult to determine (Harris 1939: 73). If so, it would be a *m.l.* for *ā*.

47. *rʾš* (line 6): **rōš*, BH *rō(ʾ)š*, "head." The *ʾalep* here is a historical spelling and was not pronounced. The development **raʾš* > *rāš* > *rōš* was completed in Palestine during the Amarna Age (Harris 1939: 42).

A Hebrew Seal
(7th century)[22]

48. *lḥmyʿdn:* **laḥamīʿaddān*, "of Ḥamiʿad-dan." The *yod* is a *m.l.* for *ī*.[23] Cf. the biblical names *ḥmyṭl (ḥ^{a}mīṭal)* and *ḥmwṭl (ḥ^{a}mūṭal)* as well as *yhwʿdn (y^{e}hōʿaddan)* (Avigad 1975: 66). On the same seal, Ḥamiʿaddan's father's name is spelled *ʾḥmlk (ʾaḥīmilk)*, without a *yod*.

The Yavneh Yam Ostracon
(7th century)[24]

49. *ʾdny* (line 1): BH *ʾ^{a}dōnī(y)*, "my lord." The *yod* is a *m.l.* for the 1s. pronoun suffix *ī*. It occurs also in *qṣry* (line 9), *ly* (lines 10, 11), *ʾty* (line 10), *nqty* (line 10), *bgdy* (line 12).

50. *ʿbdh* (line 2): **ʿabdō*, "his servant." The *he* is a *m.l.* for the 3 m.s. suffix, final *ō*.

51. *hyh* (line 3): **hayā*, "was." The *he* is a *m.l.* for a final *ā*.

52. *hywm* (line 4): "the day" or *ʾsm*, "Asam," a place name.[25] Because of the uncertainty of this reading, the word cannot be considered in the discussion.

53. *qṣrw* (line 6): **qaṣīrō*, BH *q^{e}ṣi(y)rō(w)*, "his harvest." The *waw* is a *m.l.* for the 3 m.s. possessive suffix *ō*. Cross (1962: 43, n. 31) translates this word "his harvest" but argues that the text should be restored to read *kl [ʿ]bdk ʾt qṣr<h> wʾsm*, "when thy servant had measured his harvest and had stored. . . ." He explains that "the *waw* must be construed with the following *ʾsm* in parallel to line five. Besides, the *waw* never serves as a *mater lectionis* for *ô* in this period" (cf. also Gibson 1971: 29). Although in lines 4-5, *waws* do coordinate three verbs in a sentence, *wyqṣr . . . wykl wʾsm*, a new sentence begins in line 6 with *kʾšr*.

Juxtaposing the relevant expression in lines 6-7 with its parallel in lines 8-9 suggests an alternate explanation: *kʾšr kl [ʿ]bdk ʾt qṣrw ʾsm kymm* (lines 6-7), "when *your* servant finished *his* harvest,

---

[20]Akkadian *ūmu*, "day," probably indicates that in that language a diphthong did develop which was then contracted, but this must be seen as a parallel development in East Semitic unrelated to the phonetics of Northwest Semitic Hebrew (*pace* Rainey 1972: 187). Ugaritic evidence which might be significant to this discussion is, unfortunately, inconclusive because the relevant word in the lexical texts can be read either *ia$_8$-mu* or *iú-mu* (Rainey 1972: 187).

[21]Rainey's suggestion that the contraction *aw* > *ō* may have taken place in different words in the same place at different times cannot be accepted (cf. 1972: 187, where the possibility is suggested; pp. 188-89 where it is applied to the Jerusalem dialect). The phenomenon which we call "sound change" represents a change in the articulatory habits of a speech community which affects a specific phoneme in a specific environment in every occurrence (Bloomfield 1933: 351).

Most important in Rainey's article is his observation (1972: 187) that historical spellings confuse our attempts to reconstruct ancient phonology. It is therefore necessary to have recourse to converging lines of evidence and not to base conclusions on a single inscription.

[22]Avigad 1975:66.

[23]A contemporaneous Ammonite seal with Hebrew-type names also has *y* as a *m.l.*: *ʾbyḥy (*ʾabīḥay)* (Diringer 1934: no. 103). Cf. Avigad 1952: 164, n. 2; and Bordreuil 1973: 186 *contra* Avigad 1968: 49.

[24]Naveh 1960: 129-39; Cross 1962: 42-46; *KAI* 200; II: 199-201; Gibson 1971: 26-30.

[25]The reading *ywm* was suggested by Yeivin (1962: 5) and accepted by *KAI*. Others, however, read *ʾsm*: Naveh, Cross, and Gibson.

he stored as in days past"; *kᵓšr klt ᵓt qṣry zh ymm lqḥ* (lines 8-9), . . . "when *I* finished *my* harvesting a few days ago, he [the overseer] took. . . ."[26] Both are temporal clauses in which the apodosis is not introduced by a *waw*.[27] The very same formula, *kaᵓašer killā* . . . , in BH is usually connected to its main clause by a *waw* because the verb following the *waw* is an imperfect in the narrative tense (Joüon 1923: par. 177. Cf. Gen 24:22; Deut 31:24; Judg 3:18; 8:33; but not 1 Kgs 8:54).

Pardee's discussion of the syntax (1978: 45-46) presents some additional examples of partially analogous constructions in BH. We differ in that Pardee suggests that the BH paradigm *wyhy kᵓšr . . . wy-* is also operative in lines 6-7. He accepts Cross' interpretation except that rather than restore the *m.l. he* to *qṣr* or suggest a haplography, he argues that final *m.l.* were used inconsistently in this text (1978: 46). But note that the 3 m.s. pronoun is represented (cf. datum no. 50 above).

Here, the main clauses are introduced by a verb in the past tense, and there is no reason to expect a *waw* (cf. 1 Kgs 8:54). This obviates the necessity to emend the text and points to the conclusion that the *waw* is a *m.l.*[28]

54. *hwšᶜyhw* (line 7): **hōšaᶜyahū*, a personal name. This name does not occur in the Bible. The final *waw* is a *m.l.* for *ū*, cf. also *wyᶜnw* (lines 10, 11; **wayaᶜnū*) "they will testify." The medial *waw* will be discussed in the summary below.

55. *lᵓ* (line 14 and perhaps line 12): *lō*, BH *lō(ᵓ)*, a particle of negation. Since the *ᵓalep* in this word is not etymological, it must be considered a *m.l.* for the final vowel *ō*. This spelling may have been a convention among scribes who avoided one-letter words (Tsevat 1960: 85-86, 89).

Graffiti from Khirbet el-Kôm (middle of 7th century)[29]

56. *ᶜwpy* (first inscription, line 1): **ᶜōpay* (?), a personal name, "Ophai." The name is attested in BH as the *kᵉtīb* in Jer 40:8, but its etymology is uncertain. M. Noth (1928: 230) connects it to *ᶜ-w-p*, "to fly," and translates it "Vogel," while Dever (1970: 152, n. 15) connects it to a root *ᶜ-w-p* II (< *ᶜ-y-p*; cf. *KB ad ᵓ-y-p* I) "to be dark," and translates it "Swarthy." Whatever the etymology of the name, the *waw* may be a *m.l.* for medial *ō*.[30] In his discussion of the name, however, Dever (1970: 152) notes that Greek transcriptions of the name indicate that it may have been pronounced **ᶜūpay*, in which case the *waw* might indicate a medial vowel *ū*.

57. *ntnyhw* (first inscription, line 2): **natan-yahū*, a personal name. The final *waw* is a *m.l.* for *ū*.

58. *zh* (first inscription, line 3): **zē* or **zɛ̄*, BH *zɛ̄*(h), "this." The final *he* is a *m.l.* for *ē* or *ɛ̄* (cf. no. 36).

An Inscribed Weight from Khirbet el-Kôm (7th century)[31]

59. *pym*: **pīm*. This phonetic realization of the

[26] Reading and translating the unemended text *zh ymm* with D. Pardee (1978: 43, 48-49) on the basis of BH expressions in which *zh ymm* refers to past time: 1 Sam 29:3; 2 Sam 14:2. Cf. also Amusin and Heltzer 1964: 150-51; and Gibson 1971: 29.

If emended as suggested by Cross (1962: 43) to <*k*>*ymm*, the text could be rendered "when *I* finished this *my* harvest as in days past, he took. . . ."

[27] Joüon 1923: par. 166 b, m, n. I have found no similar temporal clauses in BH in which the apodosis is not introduced by *waw*: either the so-called *waw* conversive before a verb or the conjunctive *waw* before a noun, pronoun, or interjection, e.g., *hinnē(h)*. Two temporal clauses, though not exactly of the "*kaᵓašer qatal* . . . *qatal*" pattern indicate that such a construction was possible: *hēmmā(h) rāᵓū(w) kēn tāmāhū(w) nibhᵃlū(w) neḥpāzū(w)* (Ps 48:6); *bᵉbō(w)ᵓ ᵓēlā(y)w nātān hannābī(y)ᵓ kaᵓašer bāᵓ ᵓel bat šābaᶜ* (Ps 51:2). As a type, temporal clauses are related to circumstantial and conditional clauses, which often occur in sentences in which a *waw* does not introduce the apodosis (Joüon 1923: par. 159, 167).

[28] Albright (*ANET*² Supplement: 132) rendered *ᵓt qṣrw*, "with his harvesters," parsing the second word as a plural noun with a 3 m.s. suffix. Cross (1962: 45, n. 46) was already aware of this suggestion in 1962 and objected on the grounds that the letter's author had companions, but hardly a group which he could call his harvesters. This objection still seems valid.

[29] Dever 1970. Cf. p. 150 for the dating by archeological context; p. 155 for the dating by paleography. Lemaire prefers a date closer to the end of the 8th century (1977b: 597).

[30] The *qᵉrī* in Jer 40:8, *ᶜypy (ᶜēpay)*, suggests that Dever's derivation might be preferable. The difference between the *qᵉrī* and *kᵉtīb* forms of the name could then be explained as originating in different realizations of the same name derived from dialectally differentiated forms of the same root.

[31] Dever 1970: 175 no. 8, 187. (On p. 180, par. D, the reference to "pl. IX:7; fig. 15:7" is actually to pl. IX:8; fig. 15:8.)

weight name, based on the tradition preserved in 1 Sam 13:21, indicates that the *yod* must be a *m.l.* for a medial *ī*. Were the *yod* consonantal, the reading tradition would have preserved a pronunciation **payim* < **paym* (cf. **bayit* < **bayt*). If for some reason the diphthong were contracted, a form such as **pēm* (**pē(y)m*) would have been preserved in BH.[32] Weights inscribed *p-y-m* have been found so far only in the South (Stern 1962: 870).[33]

Stamped Judean Jar Handles
(7th century)[34]

60. *zp, zyp:* **zīp*, BH *zi(y)p*, a place name. The seals with defective spellings indicate that the *yod* is a *m.l.* for *ī*.[35]

61. *šwkh: BH śōkō(h)* (one time); *śō(w)kō(h)* (three times); *śō(w)kō(w)* (three times), a place name. In BH, the name is applied to three distinct sites, Khirbet Shuweikeh in Mt. Judah (Josh 15:48; 1 Chr 4:18), Khirbet ᶜAbbād in the Shephelah (Josh 15:35; 1 Sam 17:1; 2 Chr 11:7; 28:18) and Khirbet Shuweiket in the Sharon (1 Kgs 4:10) (Aharoni 1967a: 384). The BH orthography *šwkw* is found only in post-Exilic Chronicles applied to the first and second of these sites. The orthography *škh* is used with reference to the second and third sites, while *šwkh* is employed only with reference to the first and second ones. Thus the orthography of BH is mixed, indicating that the *waw* may not be part of a historical spelling. Here, however, it will be assumed that the *waw* is etymological (cf. *EHO:* 51, no. 43 "**śawkō*"), but discussion about its phonetic realization is reserved for the summary below. The final *he* is a *m.l.* for *ō*.

Arad Ostraca
(end of 7th century)[36]

AI 31

62. ᵓ*wryhw* (line 2): *ᵓ*ūr(ī)yahū*, a personal name. Both *waws* are *m.l.* for *ū*. The orthography

---

[32]The etymology of the weight name has proved elusive. Speiser (1940: 19) proposed to relate this to Akkadian *šinipu* < Sumerian *šanabi*, "two-thirds of a shekel." His proposed etymology is possible but his concluding statement (p. 20) is problematic: "Since *šinipu*, 'two-thirds of a shekel' was analyzed as *šina* + **pû*, with the latter abstraction being understood as the word for 'a third,' the Canaanite form for the whole was naturally the dual of **pû*, i.e., *payim*." The dual form *payim* can explain the orthography of *p-y-m* but not the MT vocalization *pīm*.

Goetze (1946: 202) argued against Speiser's analysis pointing out that Akkadian *šinēpum* is composed of two components: the first *šinē* and the second, Old Babylonian *pūm*, the word for mouth. He compared this to the Hebrew idiom *pī(y) šᵉnayim* (Deut 21:17; 2 Kgs 2:9; etc.) in which the same lexical elements are found but in reverse order. Goetze concluded that the Akkadian reflects a genuine Semitic idiom and that the Sumerian form, unattested before the Old Babylonian period, must be a loan word. Dr. W. Heimpel of U. C. Berkeley informed me in 1971 that *šanabi* cannot be considered a genuine Sumerian word. These considerations, along with the observation that *šinēpu* is inflected as if derived from *pu*, encourages acceptance of Goetze's etymology (cf. von Soden 1969: par. 70i).

On the basis of these conclusions, the problem of Hebrew *p-y-m* may be resolved by assuming that the weight was borrowed along with its name either directly from Akkadian speakers or indirectly from Aramaic speakers. If directly, speakers of Hebrew must have recognized its name *pūm* as the semantic equivalent of their word for mouth, a word used in measuring expressions (Zech 13:8), and substituted for the *ū* vowel, the vowel characteristic of their word for mouth, *ī*. If indirectly, the vocalic change may have already occurred in Aramaic. As Kutscher (1976: 20-22) pointed out, in Middle Aramaic there is a clear distinction between the eastern dialects with *pwm* and the western ones with *pym, pm*, while from the orthography of Ancient, Biblical, and Elephantine Aramaic "nothing can be learnt concerning the pronunciation of the word except that it does not belong to the II-*w* class." If the *pwm-pym* distinction reflects an ancient east-west isogloss *pūm-pīm*, then the form *pīm* may be explained as an Aramaic rather than a Hebrew coinage and the vocable itself considered a loan word.

[33]W. R. Lane (1961: 21-22) believes that the weight was also employed among the Phoenicians, but since he deals only with abbreviations, *p* and *p*ᵓ, there is no way of knowing how the name was spelled or pronounced. *DISO* (225, lines 14, 17-18) questions his identification of the abbreviations with *pym*.

[34]The debate over the significance and chronology of the stamped jar handles remains unsettled. Despite disagreements concerning time of origin, there is no question that they were in use during at least some part of the 7th century. Resolution of questions affecting these stamped handles will ultimately be linked to the larger problem of archeological dating at sites such as Lachish, Arad, and Beer-Sheba. For recent discussion of the problem, cf. Aharoni 1967a: 340-46; 1973: 75-76; Cross 1969a: 20; Tushingham 1971: 25, 35; Lance 1971: 329-32; Lemaire 1975a: 678-82; Ussishkin 1976: 1-3; 1977: 56-57.

[35]Cf. Gibson 1971: 66; *AI:* 140.

[36]These come from Arad VII, whose destruction is dated to 609 B.C.E. (*AI:* 150).

of the first element should be compared with the names ᵓ*ryhw* (*AI* 26.1) and *qrb*ᵓ*wr* (*AI* 24.14), both from the 6th century.

63. ᵓ*ḥyqm* (line 5): *ᵓ*aḥīqām*, a personal name. Cf. BH ᵓ*aḥī(y)qām*. The *yod* is a *m.l.* for *ī*. Cf. ᵓ*ḥk* (*AI* 16.1; *ᵓ*aḥīkā*), "your brother," from the 6th century.

AI 32

64. *swsh:* **sūsā*, a place name. Cf. BH *ḥaṣar sū(w)sā(h)* (Josh 19:5) and *ḥaṣar sū(w)sī(y)m* (1 Chr 4:31). The *waw* is a *m.l.* for *ū*; the *he* a *m.l.* for final *ā*.

Seals from Arad
(end of 7th century)[37]

AI 105, 106, 107

65. ᵓ*lyšb* (*AI* 105, 106); ᵓ*lšb* (*AI* 107): *ᵓ*elīšāb*. All three seals were found in the same archeological context, a room identified as the archive storeroom of the fortress. The full name on the seals, ᵓ*lyšb bn* ᵓ*šyhw*, indicates that all belonged to the same individual who happens to be the addressee of many of the Arad ostraca. The orthography of the name on the third seal, without the *yod*, indicates that the *yod* in this name on the first two seals, as elsewhere in these ostraca, is a *m.l.* for *ī*, cf. BH ᵓ*ēlī(y)melek*, and ᵓ*ēlī(y)šāpāṭ*, and above no. 63.[38]

A 7th-Century Seal[39]

66. *bwzy:* **būzī*, a personal name. Cf. BH *bū(w)zī(y)*. The *waw* is a *m.l.* for *ū*; the *yod* for *ī*.

Summary and Conclusions:
Hebrew Orthography in Judah from the 8th Through the End of the 7th Centuries

All of the Hebrew epigraphic material analyzed in this section is of southern origin, and a significant amount of data is derived from inscribed materials of either monumental or official origin (Silwan, Siloam, Arad). The large number of inscriptions and their chronological and geographical congruence encourage the conclusion that their orthography is truly representative of the period in Judah.

The final vowel *ū* was represented by *waw* (44, 54, 57, 62).

The final vowel *ā* was represented by *he* (32, 33, 37, 38[?], 51, 64).

The final vowel *ā* may have been represented by ᵓ*alep* (46[?]).

The final vowel *ī* was represented by *yod* (49, 66).

The final vowel *ē* or *ε̄* was represented by *he* (19, 25, 36, 58).

The final vowel *ō* was represented by ᵓ*alep* (55).

The final vowel *ō* was represented by *he* (23, 26, 28, 38[?], 50, 61).

The final vowel *ō* was represented by *waw* (41, 53).

This use of *waw* as a *m.l.* may be explained by reference to the phonetic and orthographic situation which must have prevailed in southern Hebrew toward the end of the 8th century.

During the 8th century, the contraction of *aw* > *ō* in unaccented syllables, which is attested in Phoenician, Moabite,[41] and Israelite Hebrew (no. 7) eventually reached Judah (no. 17). Its dissemination in Judean Hebrew (nos. 35, 42, 43)[42] may have been accelerated through the influence of the speech habits of northern refugees fleeing the civil disorder and Assyrian devastation of their kingdom.[43] Where the contraction took place,

---

[37]*AI:* 121.

[38]Cf. the defective spelling on an Ammonite seal of ᵓ*lš*ᶜ (*ᵓ*ēlīša*ᶜ), published by Galling, *ZDPV* 64 (1941), 191, no. 128 (cited in Bordreuil and Lemaire 1974: 33 n. 9). Herr (1978: 85) dates the defectively written seal later than the *plene* ones on paleographic grounds.

[39]Diringer 1934: no. 31. The provenience of this seal is unknown. Since it was acquired in Jerusalem, I am assuming that it is of southern origin.

[40]*KAI* 26: *mmṣ*ᵓ (lines 4 ff.) < *wṣ*ᵓ = BH *mō(w)ṣā*ᵓ; *wyšb* (line 11) < *wšb*, a Phoenician *Yipil*, **yōšib*, = BH *hō(w)šī(y)b*.

[41]*KAI* 181: *hš*ᶜ*ny* (line 4) < *wš*ᶜ = BH **hō(w)šī(y)*ᶜ*ēnī(y)* [this form is attested in BH only as an imperative, not in the perfect conjugation]; ᵓ*šb* (line 13) < *wšb* = BH *ᵓ*ō(w)šī(y)b* [attested only in ᵓ*ō(w)ši(y)b*ᵉ*kā* (Hos 12:10)].

[42]Nos. 42, 43 constitute corroborating evidence only if they are derived from II-*waw* nouns.

[43]Rainey (1972: 189) notes that the Akkadian transcription of the name of Hoshea, the northern monarch who reigned in 731 B.C.E. is ᵐ*A-ú-si-*ᵓ*a* whereas the same name is written ᵐ*Ú-si-a* (from Assur), and ᵐ*Ú-si-*ᵓ*a* (from Gozan) in documents written

originally consonantal *waws* which were retained as being part of the conventional orthography of certain words were taken as *m.l.* for $\bar{o}$. At times this usage was extended to indicate the same vowel where there may not have been an etymological *w* (no. 34) (a usage attested in 7th-century Ammonite orthography);[44] and at times it was omitted from the orthography of words in which *w* was an etymological phone (35, 42[?], 43[?]). Having evolved into a *m.l.* by virtue of new habits of pronunciation being imposed on texts composed in a conventional orthography, *waw* as a *m.l.* for $\bar{o}$ was extended by innovative scribes to nonmedial positions.

In final position, the grapheme *he* was used to indicate consonantal *h* in a few "third gutteral" verbs (*gbh, kmh, mhh, ngh, tmh*)[45] and in the 3 f.s. pronominal suffix. It also was used to indicate the vowels $\bar{a}$, $\bar{e}$ (or $\bar{\varepsilon}$), and $\bar{o}$ in word final position. Although context most likely determined which of the theoretically many phonetic values was to be assigned the *he*, in some situations ambiguity may have remained. By employing *waw* as a *m.l.* for $\bar{o}$ in word final positions, some potential ambiguities were eliminated. When employed to mark the 3 m.s. pronominal suffix $\bar{o}$, it graphically distinguished between the masculine and feminine suffixes. Moreover, in this position there was small opportunity for confusion between *waw* as a *m.l.* for $\bar{o}$ and as a *m.l.* for $\bar{u}$, because the first value would occur exclusively with substantives, while the second, most frequently with verbs.

The medial vowel $\bar{u}$ was represented by *waw* (29, 56[?], 62, 64, 66).

The medial vowel $\bar{\imath}$ was represented by *yod* (31, 48, 59, 60, 63, 65).

The medial vowel $\bar{o}$ was represented by *ʾalep* (27, 47).

The medial vowel $\bar{o}$ was represented by *waw* (22, 34, 39, 46, 54, 56[?], 61).[46]

One datum may be interpreted to indicate that in unaccented syllables the diphthong *ay* was contracted to $\bar{e}$ (no. 30), which in turn would imply that the *yod* in *yyn* (no. 21) might be a *m.l.* for $\bar{e}$.[47] The datum, however, is problematic (cf. n. 12) so that additional corroborating evidence is necessary before this conclusion can be drawn safely.

---

ca. 611 B.C.E. The first spelling is taken to indicate that the contraction of the diphthong had not yet taken place, whereas the second two spellings are taken to indicate that it was well established in the Hebrew of the Northern exiles. If his conclusion that [m]*A-ú-si-ʾa* reflects an uncontracted diphthong is correct, then evidence relating to Northern Hebrew would indicate that the contraction of the diphthong in unaccented syllables was a protracted process extending from the end of the 9th through the middle of the 8th centuries (cf. above no. 3). Attestation of the contracted diphthong in two distinct communities of northern exiles permits the assumption that these communities preserved a linguistic pattern which was completely developed before their exile, ca. 722 B.C.E.

[44] *Waw* is attested as a *m.l.* for $\bar{o}$ in the Ammonite name *šwḥr*, a participial form. Cf. Bordreuil 1973: 182; Avigad 1970: 286-87. Avigad incorrectly transcribes the name as *Shawḥer* and translates it "Shôḥer." His transcription indicates that the *waw* was consonantal, forming a diphthong which was contracted. The *Qal* participial pattern in BH, and presumably in Ammonite, was $C\bar{o}CvC < C\bar{a}CvC$, where $\bar{o}$ was a pure vowel.

[45] None of these infrequent BH verbs are attested yet in any known Hebrew inscriptions from the biblical period.

[46] Cf. the preceding discussion of *waw* as a *m.l.* for final $\bar{o}$.

[47] Cf. our conclusions concerning northern orthography of the 8th century B.C.E. above pp. 14-15.

Chapter 4
The Sixth Century

A Hebrew Seal
(end of 7th-beginning of 6th century)[1]

67. *yhwʾḥz:* **yahōʾāḥāz*, a personal name. Cf. BH *yᵉhō(w)ʾāḥāz*. The *waw* is a medial *m.l.* for *ō*.

A Hebrew Seal
(early 6th century)[2]

68. *ḥwrṣ:* **ḥōrēṣ*, a personal name. This name, not attested elsewhere in the Hebrew onomasticon, is a participial formation derived from one of the homonymous and homographic roots *ḥ-r-ṣ* (cf. *BDB* and *KB ad ḥrṣ*), but its meaning is not clear. Whatever its meaning, the *waw* is not etymological and must be an internal *m.l.* for the vowel *ō* (cf. chap. 3, n. 44).

Ostraca from Arad
(early 6th century)[3]

AI 1

69. *yyn* (line 3): **yayin*, "wine." The noun occurs here in the absolute state; however, in line 9, the same orthography occurs when the noun is in a bound construction where massoretic vocalization indicates that the diphthong had contracted in the unaccented syllable (cf. below *ad* no. 101).

70. *hym* (line 4): **hayyōm*, "the day." Cf. above, no. 43.

71. *ʿwd* (line 5; cf. also 5.3; 21.8):[4] **ʿōd*, "remainder." For the status of the *waw* as a *m.l.* for *ō*, cf. the discussion above on the use of medial and final *waw* in 7th-century orthography.

AI 3

72. *ʾlk* (line 9): **ʾēlēkā* or **ēlɛ̄kā*, "to yourself." The orthography of this word offers indirect evidence for the contraction of the diphthong *ay* in unaccented syllables. The base form of this preposition is **ʾly*, and with the 2 m.s. suffix, the reconstructed form appears to have been *ʾlyk* *(*ʾēláyka)*. Cf. BH *ʾēlɛ̄(y)ka*. The contraction exhibited in the massoretic tradition and the nonconsonantal *yod* which remains persistently in the BH orthography of this form cannot be readily explained as deriving from the contraction of the diphthong in an accented syllable. Rather, it must be assumed that the contraction occurred in forms of the preposition with heavy suffixes, i.e., **ʾalaykím* > **ʾalēkím*, BH *ʾᵃlēkɛ̄m*, which was then analogically assumed by other forms in the paradigm.[5] The form in this ostracon represents a

---

[1]Avigad 1969: 9.
[2]Avigad 1970: 287. Cf. F. Vattioni 1969: 22.
[3]Cited from *AI*.
[4]In 2.7, the meaning of the vocable *ʿwd* is not clear; it may be a verb, **ʿiwwēd*, meaning "to be extra."
[5]In BH the following forms occur both with and without a *yod: ʾlkm/ ʾlykm; ʾlhm/ ʾlyhm; ʾlhn/ ʾlyhn.*

phonetic spelling after the analogous contraction had taken place.[6]

AI 7

73. *ššh* (line 4): **šiššā*, "six." The *he* is a final *m.l.* for *ā*.

74. *ktbth* (line 6): **katabtā*, "you wrote." The *he* is a final *m.l.* for *ā*.

75. *lp̊nẙk* (line 6): **lapanēkā*, BH *lᵉpānε̄(y)kā*, "before you." The basic form of the preposition is *l* + *pny* and the situation is analogous to that discussed above in no. 72. Assuming that the conclusion reached there is correct, the orthography of this word must be considered historical and the *yod* regarded as a *m.l.* for a medial *ē* or .

AI 16

76. *ʾḥk* (line 1): **ʾaḥīkā*, "your brother." There are no *m.l.* in this word. The vowel *ī* is not indicated by *yod* in the orthography in the middle of the word.

77. *brktk* (lines 2-3): **bēraktīkā*, "I blessed you." As in the preceding example, the vowel *ī*, here marking a pronominal suffix, is not indicated by *yod* in the middle of the word.

78. *šlḥty* (line 4): **šalaḥtī*, "I sent." *Yod* is a *m.l.* for the suffixed pronominal morpheme *ī*.

79. *yhwh* (line 6): **yahwē*, the divine name. The final *he* is a *m.l.* for *ē* or *ε̄*. Cf. also *AI* 18.2, 9 and Lachish 2.2.[7]

AI 17

80. *byth* (line 2): **baytā*, "to the house." The *he* is the so-called *he locale*.[8] There is no evidence which suggests that this *he* was consonantal in BH; it may therefore be concluded that it is a *m.l.* for the final vowel *ā*.

81. *mhrh* (line 5): **mahērā*, BH *mᵉhērā(h)*, "quickly." The second *he* is a *m.l.* for final *ā*.

82. *ʾth* (line 6): **ʾōtō*, "it" (the direct object). The *he* is a *m.l.* for final *ō*.

AI 18

83. *ʾdny* (line 1): **ʾadōnī*, "my lord." The *yod* is a *m.l.* for final *ī*. Cf. also *ṣwtny* (lines 7-8; **ṣiwwitanī*), "you commanded me."

84. *šmryhw* (line 4): **šamaryahū*, a personal name. The final *waw* is a *m.l.* for *ū*.

85. *hʾ* (line 10): **hūʾ*, or **hū*. The status of the final *ʾalep* is uncertain. It should be noted that *waw* is not used to mark the medial vowel *ū* (cf. the note to no. 109).

AI 24

86. *qrbʾwr* (line 14): **qarabʾūr*, a personal name not attested elsewhere. The *waw* is a medial *m.l.* for *ū*. Cf. the orthography of the same onomastic element in the name *ʾryhw* (*AI* 26.1; **ʾūryahū*) on an ostracon dated paleographically to the 6th century. Cf. above, no. 62.

87. *hbqydm* (lines 14-15): **hibqīdām*, "he shall hand them over." The root of this word is *b-q-d*, a dialectal variant of commonly attested BH *p-q-d*. The *yod* is a medial *m.l.* for *ī*, in this case the characteristic vowel of the *Hipʿil* conjugation.

88. *yqrh* (line 16): **yiqrē*, BH *yiqrε̄(h)*, "happen." The final *he* is a *m.l.* for *ē* or *ε̄* .

89. *hʿyr* (line 17): **haʿīr*, "the city." The *yod* is most likely a medial *m.l.* for *ī*.[9]

90. *lhʿyd* (line 18): **lahaʿīd*, "to testify." As in no. 86, the *yod* is a *m.l.* for the medial vowel *ī* characteristic of the *Hipʿil* conjugation.

---

[6] If the word on the ostracon is *ʾlkm*, then the orthography of the form is a direct attestation to the contraction.

[7] For the enumeration of the Lachish letters, cf. below, pp. 29-30, and n. 11.

[8] *AI ad loc.* Aharoni cites as corroborative evidence Judg 18:18; Gen 28:2; 43:17, 24; 44:14; 47:14.

[9] Cross and Freedman (*EHO:* 55) write: "The *yod* may be an internal *mater lectionis*. . . . Nevertheless, a variant form is possible, **ʿayr* or the like. Compare the plural forms *ʿārīm* and *ʿᵃyārīm* (?) Judg 10:4."

The first plural form which they cite, the regular discontinuous plural of *ʿīr*, is irrelevant to the discussion since it contains no *yod* as a second radical and the putative singular from which it is formed, **ʿar*, is a biradical noun. (Cf. BH *ʿār*, an area in Moab, Num 21:28; Deut 2:18; etc.) The second plural form which they cite is highly doubtful, as they indicate with the question mark. It may be either a scribal error or a conscious deformation of the plural for the sake of a pun on *ʿᵃyārīm*, the plural of *ʿayir*/*ʿīr* (Gen 49:11), "male ass."

The etymology of *ʿi(y)r* is unknown.

An Ostracon from Arad
(early 6th century)[10]

91. *hsws:* **hasūs*, "the horse." The *waw* is a *m.l.* for the medial vowel *ū*.

The Lachish Letters
(early 6th century)[11]

92. *ᵓdny* (2.1 = *KAI* 192.1): **ᵓadōnī*, BH *ᵓᵃdōnī(y)*, "my lord." The *yod* is a *m.l.* for the final vowel *ī*.

93. *yᵓwš* (2.1 = *KAI* 192.1): **yaᵓūš* or **yaᵓōš*, a proper name. The name is to be explained as a *Qal* jussive of **ᵓūš* (= *ᵓ-w-š*), "to give a gift" (cf. Ugaritic *ušn* and ESA *ᵓws*), and the *waw* must be a medial *m.l.* for either *ū* or *ō*.[12]

94. *my* (2.3 = *KAI* 192.3): **mī*, "who," BH *mī(y)*. The *yod* is a *m.l.* for the final vowel *ī*. Cf. also *ky* (2.2 = *KAI* 192.3; **kī*), "because."

95. *ᶜ]bdh* (2.5 = *KAI* 192.5): **ᶜabdō*, "his servant." The *he* is a *m.l.* for final *ō*.

96. *lᵓ* (2.6 = *KAI* 192.6): **lō*, BH *lō(ᵓ)*, "no." The *ᵓalep* is not etymological and is a *m.l.* for *ō*.

97. *ᵓyš* (3.9-10 = *KAI* 193.9-10): **ᵓīš*, "man." The *yod* is a *m.l.* for *ī*.

98. *mṣrymh* (3.16 = *KAI* 193.16): **miṣraymā*, "to Egypt." The diphthong *ay* is not contracted in an accented syllable. The *he* is a *m.l.* for a final vowel *ā*. Cf. no. 80, above.

99. *ᵓnšw* (3.18 = *KAI* 193.18): "his men." This form may be explained in two different ways: 1) *ᵓnš* may be regarded as a morphologically singular collective noun with a regular 3 m.s. possessive suffix *ō*, i.e., **ᵓanōšō*. The collective sense of BH *ᵓᵉnōš* is found in Isa 24:6, where the word is parallel to *yōšᵉbē(y) ᵓereṣ*, "dwellers in the land," and perhaps in the *kᵉtīb*, *ᵓnšw*, "his men," at 1 Sam 23:5. Cf. *ḥayil* (2 Sam 24:4; 2 Kgs 24:14) and *ḥᵃyālīm* (2 Kgs 25:23; 2 Chr 16:4); *ṣābā(ᵓ)* (2 Sam 2:8; 1 Chr 25:1) and *ṣᵉbāᵓō(w)t* (Deut 20:9). If this is the proper explanation, then *waw* is a *m.l.* for a final *ō*, the 3 m.s. possessive suffix added to singular nouns. 2) It may be explained as a plural noun with a 3 m.s. possessive suffix, BH *ᵓᵃnāšā(y)w*. At Lachish, it may have been pronounced **ᵓanāšāw*.[13] This form of the suffix may be derived as follows: *áyhū* > *áyū* or *áyō* (syncope of *h* [perhaps indicated orthographically as *yh*, cf. Lemaire 1977b: 599 and the note to datum 26]) >*ā̃w* (syncope or assimilation of *y* and compensatory lengthening of the vowel; *EHO:* 68; Blau 1976: 24, par. 7.1.6). In BH, the diphthong *ay* in an accented syllable generally remains uncontracted and there is no epigraphic evidence to suggest that it was contracted in Judean Hebrew from the 7th century on.[14] The Lachish spelling without *yod* would

[10]Rainey 1977: 99. This ostracon will be no. 111 in the English version of *AI*. For the date, cf. p. 97.

[11]*EHO:* 46 and the literature cited there; *KAI* II: 189-90. The date of 917 B.C.E. suggested by N. R. Ganor (1967: 74-77) is based on his acceptance of the statement by N. H. Torczyner, who first edited the letters, that the "script of the ostraca seems to be identical with that of the Meša tablet which is 250 years earlier than the ostraca." Torczyner was wrong in his paleographic analysis, as any recent chart comparing the scripts, or for that matter, the chart published in the official volume edited by Torczyner himself, will reveal (1938: opposite p. 220). Even in Ganor's translation of Torczyner's statement (from Torczyner 1939: 30), the word "seem" qualifies the statement. Ganor, however, latched on to the word "identical" and constructed his theory with no reference to recent advances in paleography.

The letters are cited both according to their numbering and lineation in Torczyner 1938 and according to their numbers in *KAI*.

[12]Cross and Freedman (*EHO:* 51-52) explain this orthography as a hybrid resulting from the impact of popular speech on historic spelling. Supposedly the historical spelling was *yᵓš* (**yaᵓōš*). At Lachish this name was pronounced **yawš*, i.e., *aᵓo* > *aw*, which if spelled phonetically would have yielded *ywš*. The Lachish spelling represents a combination of these forms. Underlying this explanation, of course, is the assumption that *waw* cannot be a *m.l.* for *ō*.

In his review of *EHO*, W. Moran (1953: 366) remained unconvinced by the authors' explanation of this orthography, pointing to the identical orthography in the ESA name *yᵓwsᵓl*, which cannot be explained by recourse to the quiescence of the *ᵓalep* and formation of the diphthong. The orthography of the ESA name has since been happily explained as the regular imperfect of a *media infirma* verb with a *plene* spelling (Beeston 1962: 27).

[13]Cross and Freedman (*EHO:* 54) suggest that it may have been vocalized *ᵓanašaw* in Judahite Hebrew. If so, then the diphthong must have developed after the contraction *áw* > *ō̃* in the form of the suffix attached to singular nouns had taken place; otherwise, both would have become *ō*. However, in their excursus on "Orthographic Problems in the Massoretic Text" (*EHO:* 68, n. 21), they write that "the form in the Lachish Letters may be read either **ᵓāw* or **êw*."

[14]The phonology and orthography of plural nouns with possessive pronominal suffixes in BH indicate that with singular suffixes the accented diphthong remained uncontracted; but with plural suffixes, the diphthong contracted because the heavy

indicate that the orthography of this suffix in the MT with *yod* may not necessarily be an actual historical spelling.[15]

100. *šlḥh* (3.21 = *KAI* 193.21): **šalaḥō*, "he sent it." The *he* is a *m.l.* for *ō* here and in *lqḥh* (4.6 = *KAI* 194.6), "he took him."

101. *byt hrpd* (4.5 = *KAI* 194.5): **bēt* (?), "house of." Cf. BH *bē(y)t*. Indirect evidence attesting to the contraction of the diphthong *ay* in unaccented syllables has been discussed above (nos. 72, 75, and 30 [the last example stemming from the preceding century]). There is, however, a distinction important to consider between this and the preceding examples. In nos. 30, 72, and 75, the contraction resulted in the formation of an open syllable, whereas here the purportedly resultant form is a closed syllable. This difference in linguistic environments precludes drawing inferences from the former examples.[16]

102. *wyʿlhw* (4.6-7 = *KAI* 194.6-7): **wayyaʿalēhū*, BH *wayyaʿălēhū(w)*, "he has taken him up." The final *waw* is a *m.l.* for *ū*.

103. *hʿyrh* (4.7 = *KAI* 194.7): **haʿīrā*, "to the city." The *yod* is most likely a medial *m.l.* for *ī*; the second *he* a final *m.l.* for *ā*. Cf. no. 89, above.

104. *spry* (6.4 = *KAI* 196.4): **siprē* (?) "letters of." If the conclusions reached in the discussion of no. 72 are correct, then the *yod* here is a *m.l.* for *ē*. Cf. also *dbry* (6.6; **dibrē* [?]), "words of"; *ydyk* (6.6; **yadēkā*), "your hands" (cf. BH *yādɛ̄(y)kā).*

105. *htšʿyt* (20.1, not in *KAI*): **hatišīʿīt*, "the ninth." Cf. BH *tĕšīʿī(y)t*. The *yod* is a *m.l.* for *ī*. Cf. *AI* 20.1, from the 6th century, *bšlšt* (**bašalīšīt*), "on the third day," where the same suffix is spelled without a *yod*.

106. *ʾkzy[b]:*[17] **ʾakzīb*, a place name. Cf. BH *ʾakzī(y)b*. If the restoration is correct, the *yod* is a *m.l.* for *ī*.

Inscriptions from Khirbet Beit Lei (6th century)[18]

107. *ʾwrr* (fig. 10; pl. 11 E, F): **ʾōrēr*, "a curser." If not an error for *ʾrwr (*ʾārūr)*, "cursed," the inscribed form is the active participle and the *waw* a *m.l.* for *ō*.[19]

108. *yhd* (A, line 2): **yahūdā* or **yāhūd*, a place name. The orthography contains no *m.l.*[20]

109. *lw* (A, line 2): **lō*, BH *lō(w)*, "to him" (cf.

---

suffixes themselves were accented (cf. no. 30, above). The contracted diphthong was then extended by analogy to plural nouns before the 1st plural suffix *-nū*, even though it is accented.

[15]The *yod* may have been reintroduced into the orthography of the suffix on the analogy of the rest of the paradigm, in order to indicate the plurality of the noun. Cf. Zevit 1977: 328, n. 63.

[16]Indirect attestation that the *ay* > *ē* contraction took place in this environment by the 5th century B.C.E. is found in the Akkadian orthography of the theophorous element *bētʾēl* in the Murašu documents from Nippur (Coogan 1976: 48, 107). However, although the contraction is indicated, there is no evidence that the names were those of Hebrew speakers who pronounced them in southern dialect.

Coogan (117, n. 32) suggests that the contraction first took place in the Mesopotamian Aramaic with which the Judean exiles came into contact and that it influenced their pronunciation of Hebrew. The contraction, in turn, was reintroduced into Judah by some of the returnees. This is not an impossible hypothesis, though the linguistic dynamics presupposed are surely in need of clarification and some concrete examples are definitely called for.

[17]Found on an ostracon at Lachish and dated to the end of the Judean monarchy (Aharoni 1968: 168).

[18]For this date cf. Naveh 1968: 74, n. 38; Cross 1970: 304. The inscriptions were originally published by J. Naveh in 1963 (92), where a date ca. 700 B.C.E. was assigned to them. The inscriptions are cited here according to their enumeration in Naveh 1963.

[19]In BH all three occurrences of this form are spelled without the *waw* (Gen 27:29; Num 24:9; Job 3:8).

[20]F. M. Cross (1970: 301) reads this word *yhdh* where J. Naveh reads *yhd* and rejects the reading of the following word *lw* (our no. 109) as impossible because "*waw* does not become a vowel letter for *ô* before the fourth century in Hebrew." He reads the *lamed* of *lw* as a *he* belonging to the preceding word, hence *yhdh*, while he treats the *waw* as the conjunction prefixed to the following word, i.e., *wgʾlty* where Naveh reads *lʾlhy*.

The downstroke of the *he* which Cross notes as "faint but clear enough" is not attached to the horizontal bars but is off to their right, branching off of a zig-zag scratch which starts above the first line and extends to below the second. (Cross' drawing appears to bring the downstroke closer to the putative head of the *he* than Naveh's photograph indicates.) Furthermore, the sharp angle formed by the disputed strokes, which he points out as characteristic of 6th century *he* (305, n. 8), is not found on the other *he*s in these inscriptions but is found on some of the *lamed*s.

A. Lemaire (1976: 558-60) reads *yhwdh . lʾlhy* with a medial *waw* (= *m.l.* for *ū*) in the place name, followed by a *he* or a *taw*, and a word divider. I am unable to discern the medial *waw* which he sees. The *he* has been discussed above, while his word divider is a

n. 20). The *waw* is a final *m.l.* for the 3 m.s. pronominal suffix *ō*.[21]

Summary and Conclusions:
Hebrew Orthography of the 6th Century

The epigraphic material dated to this century which was examined above is, with the possible exception of two seals, of southern origin. In addition, almost all of the data were found at two locations: Arad and Lachish.[22] The ostraca from these sites do not reflect the local scribal traditions since they were composed elsewhere. Nevertheless, because of their official nature, it may be assumed that both sets of ostraca conformed to the parameters of what was considered "standard" or "normalized" orthography. The two collections offer evidence that limited orthographic variations were tolerated in official correspondence. At Arad, the *yod* was found to indicate the characteristic long vowel of the *Hipᶜil* conjugation (nos. 87, 90), whereas in the ostraca unearthed at Lachish the vowel was not so indicated: *lhg[d]* (3.1-2 = *KAI* 193.1-2; **lahaggīd*), "to tell"; *hšb* (5.6 = *KAI* 195.6; **hēšīb*), "he returned."

Allowing for some local variations as well as individual idiosyncrasies, the uses of *m.l.* in the 6th century may be described as follows:

The final vowel *ū* was represented by *waw* (84, 102).

The final vowel *ā* was represented by *he* (73, 74, 80, 81, 98, 103).

The final vowel *ī* was represented by *yod* (78, 83, 92, 94).

The final vowel *ē* or *ε̄* was represented by *he* (79, 88).

The final vowel *ē* was represented by *yod* (104 [?]).

The final vowel *ō* was represented by *ᵓalep* (96).

The final vowel *ō* was represented by *he* (82, 95, 100).

The final vowel *ō* was represented by *waw* (99 [?], 109).

The final vowel *ū* was represented by *ᵓalep* (85 [?]).

The medial vowel *ū* was represented by *waw* (86, 91, 93[?], 107[?]).

The medial vowel *ī* was represented by *yod* (87, 89, 90, 97, 103, 105, 106[?]).

The medial vowel *ō* was represented by *waw* (67, 68, 71, 93[?], 107).

The medial vowel *ē* or *ε̄* was represented by *yod* (75, 101).

A comparison of these uses of *m.l.* with those of the preceding century reveals that, except for the wider extension of *yod* as a medial *m.l.* for *ī*, no innovations took place. Furthermore, in light of the stability of the orthography during these two centuries, it is possible to speak about Judahite scribal practices in general.[23]

Data from this century also bear on the history of the 2 m.s. form of perfect verbs. Both at Arad and at Lachish the suffix is attested with *plene* orthography: *AI* 7.6, *ktbth* (**katabtā*), "you wrote"; 40.9, *ydᶜth*, (**yadaᶜtā*), "you knew"; Lachish 2.6 = *KAI* 192.6, *ydᶜth* (**yadaᶜtā*), "you knew"; and the same word again, perhaps with the same sense, in 3.8 = *KAI* 193.8. These invite contrast with the 2 m.s. *qṭl*-forms preceded by the so-called "*waw*-conversive" which are all written defectively: *AI* 2.5-6, *whsbt* (**wahēsabtā*), "you will 'inspect' (?)"; 2.8, *wntt* (**wanātattā*), "you will give"; 3.5, *wṣrrt* (**waṣarartā*), "you will bind/load up"; 3.8 and 17.3-4, *wlqḥt* (**walaqaḥtā*), "you will take."[24]

---

waw. Comparison of the disputed sign with the size, stance, and spacing of the divider before the last word, *yršlm*, makes this clear. For these reasons, I prefer to follow Naveh's readings at this point.

[21]It is already so employed in the 8th-century Aramaic Panamu inscription from Zenjirli, *KAI* 215.11: *ᵓ]by. lw. bᶜl. ksp. hw. wlw. bᶜl. zhb*, "My father was not an owner of silver and not an owner of gold. . . ."

[22]Khirbet Beit Lei is located five miles east of Lachish.

[23]N. H. Torczyner (1938: 15, 17) argues that the Lachish letters originated at Qiryat Yearim and at Jerusalem, while Aharoni (1970: 25, 28) argues that the Arad ostraca originated at different places in the south including Arad itself. In addition, the presence of graffiti indicates that by the 7th century, writing had spread beyond scribal circles (Naveh 1970a: 279).

[24]This distinction was first noted by H. V. D. Parunak (1978: 26), who, however, viewed the defective orthography in these examples as well as in examples of the 2 m.s. possessive suffix *-k* as an indication that no vowel was pronounced here. (The 2 m.s. suffix is discussed in chap. 1, pp. 9-10.)

Parunak's translation of *AI* 7.6, *ktbth lpnyk*, "write it before you," is the key to his argument that the *he* in the Arad examples of

This orthographic distinction between the two forms may have been due to the marked accentual difference between them which is partially preserved in the massoretic traditions: *qāṭáltā* vs. *(wᵉ)qāṭaltā́*. As the accentual distinction between these forms disappeared due to the infrequency and disuse of the *qṭl*-future tense, the *defective* orthography tended to prevail. This process most likely occurred after the 6th century.

BH preserves a number of examples where the suffix is still found *plene* in a pre-Exilic text but *defective* in its post-Exilic parallel: *glyth* (2 Sam 7:27) // *glyt* (1 Chr 17:25); *whyth* (2 Sam 10:11) // *whyyt* (1 Chr 19:12); *wnplth* (2 Kgs 14:10) // *wnplt* (2 Chr 25:19).[25]

Comparison of these data with those from 8th-century Israel is of little value. The material bearing on Israelite orthography offers little in the way of continuous text and is too fragmentary and scattered to allow a *synthetic* description of northern scribal traditions. For these reasons, the following discussion is restricted to southern orthography of the two centuries preceding the Exile.

Assuming that the practices of those who wrote the inscriptions, letters, graffiti, and seals were the same as those of the authors of court chronicles, laws, and psalms in Jerusalem, then the latter also did the following: 1) indicated long final vowels in the orthography; 2) indicated long medial vowels which developed from the diphthongs *aw* or *ay*, i.e., maintained historical spellings; 3) indicated long vowels in medial positions when the *m.l.* was not a historical spelling in certain nouns, e.g., *ʾyš*, and grammatical forms, e.g., *Qal* participles, *Hipʿil* verbs; 4) indicated the 3 m.s. possessive pronominal suffix sporadically by *waw* rather than by *he*; 5) did not indicate medial short vowels by any *m.l.* Biblical texts composed during this period would have been written in accord with these orthographic conventions, while texts composed in the earlier defective orthography could have been rewritten or have had certain obscure points and ambiguities cleared up in accord with them.

---

this suffix marks an object. The lines in question, lines 6-8, should, however, be translated "you wrote in front of yourself (i.e., you wrote down): 'on the second of the month' in the tenth (month)." *ʾlyšb* is being informed that his records are incorrect regarding the day of the tenth month on which he is to provision the Kittim. Lines 2-5 contain the proper instructions: "Give to the Kittim for the tenth (month) from (the period of) the first to the sixth of the month three baths."

[25]There is also an example of the late source preserving the early orthography: *wntth* (2 Chr 6:30) // *wntt* (1 Kgs 8:39). Cf. also Gen 21:23, *wgrth*; Exod 18:20, *whzhrth;* and Sperber 1939: 181-82. The *plene* orthography which appears commonly at Qumran must be considered independent of the pre-Exilic conventions being discussed here. For data drawn from 1QIsaª, cf. Kutscher 1974: 440-41.

Chapter 5
After the Sixth Century

During the Exilic and post-Exilic periods innovations characteristic of MT orthography were introduced. These are partially documented in fragments of biblical texts from Qumrân dated paleographically to the 3rd century B.C.E. (4QExod[f] and 4QJer[a]; cf. Freedman 1962: 96-101). *Waw* almost completely replaced *he* as a *m.l.* for the 3 m.s. possessive suffix with singular nouns[1] and *yod* was utilized as a graphic device[2] to indicate when the suffixed noun was plural and the attached pronoun was to be pronounced *āw* and not *ō*[3]. *Yod* was also used to indicate the vowel *ī* in some forms of the *Hipᶜil* conjugation, in some common nouns, e.g., *ᵓyš* (**ᵓīš*), and in the masculine plural suffix *īm*. *He* ceased to be employed as a *m.l.* for the final vowel *ā* of the 2 m.s. suffix of verbs in the perfect. The popularity and prestige of these innovations are indicated by the fact that scribal activity has *almost* obliterated all traces of earlier orthography from the MT.

In addition, certain secondary usages were introduced. *Waw* was employed with substantives to indicate the *ō* vowel characteristic of the *Qal* active participle of transitive verbs (cf. nos. 68, 107); the feminine plural ending *ōt* (cf. no. 34); the numerals *šlwš* (**šālōš*), "three," and *šmwnh* (**šᵉmōnɛ̄*), "eight"; and in certain nouns such as *bkwr* (**bᵉkōr*), "firstborn," and *mᶜwz* (**māᶜōz*), "stronghold." Similarly, it was used to indicate the vowel *ō* in some forms of the triliteral verb: *ldrwš*[4] (**lidᵉrōš*), "to seek," *tšmwr*[5], (**tišmōr*), "you watch," as well as in forms of verbs with a stem vowel *ō* or *ū*, i.e., hollow verbs.[6] Considered phonetically, the data indicate that the use of *waw* as a *m.l.* was extended from *ō* < *aw* to *ō* < *á̄* and to *ō* < *u*.

---

[1]More than 50 cases of spelling with an original *he* are still found in the *kᵉtīb* of the MT, and of these 15 involve the word *klh* (*kᵉtīb*), *kullō* (*qᵉrī*) (Gordis 1937: 92-94).

B. Porten (1971: 326-28) points out that the divine name written independently or as a theophoric element in personal names was spelled *yhh* at Elephantine in Egypt by scribes who wrote or who were trained in the first quarter of the 5th century B.C.E., i.e., 500-475: *yhh, yhhrm*. From the fact that *he* was not used as a *m.l.* for *ō* in Aramaic, Porten deduces that this reflects a Hebrew spelling convention. From 460 on, the spelling *yhh* was replaced by *yhw*, a change attributed by Porten to the influence of Aramaic spelling conventions; but might this not also be explained as reflecting the change in Hebrew conventions when *waw* replaced *he* as a *m.l.* for *ō* in final position? For the evidence that *he* in *yhh* was a *m.l.* for *ō*, cf. p. 328.

[2]Cf. the discussion of no. 99, above.

[3]There are more than 100 cases in the *kᵉtīb-qᵉrī* notations alone where the original orthography of the suffix with a plural noun is preserved: Deut 2:33; 7:9; 1 Sam 2:9, 10; 3:2, 18, etc. (Gordis 1937: 86-91).

[4]Construct Infinitive. Cf. 2 Chr 12:14.

[5]Imperfect. Cf. 1 Chr 22:13; 2 Chr 7:17.

[6]The data in this paragraph are based on the groupings suggested by Murtonen (1953: 48) and as emended by him in 1973-74: 67-68.

The developments adumbrated in the preceding paragraph did not attain the prestige of the earlier innovations and were therefore applied with less rigor (cf. Sperber 1943: 162-76). Thus, they are more characteristic of Exilic and post-Exilic books than of pre-Exilic ones. But within the latter, they are more characteristic of late material or of early material which was orthographically revised and reedited after the Exile than of material whose consonantal text was not subjected to this process.[7]

Moreover, research into the application of secondary usages in the biblical text indicates that they occur under grammatically definable conditions in relatively few categories of words (Murtonen 1973-74: 67; Cohen 1975: 60-66; 1976: 362). For example, in Genesis, within forms of the verb *bōʾ*, "to come," in which the *ō* vowel occurs, it is represented by the *m.l.* only in certain forms. The following are the data reflecting the *plene* (= p) or *defective* (= d) orthography of this verb in *Qal:*

Infinitive absolute: bwʾ—3p, 0d;
Construct infinitive: bbw—1p, 0d; *kbwʾ*—1p, 0d; *lbwʾ*—6p, 1d; *bʾy*—0p, 1d; *bbʾy*—0p, 1d; *kbʾy*—0p, 1d; *bʾk(h)*—0p, 4d; *bbʾk*—0p, 0d; *bbʾw*—0p, 2d; *bʾkm*—0p, 0d; *bʾm*—0p, 1d; *bbʾn(h)*—0p, 1d;
Imperative: bʾ—1p, 4d; *bʾy*—0p, 1d; *bʾw*—0p,
Imperfect: ʾbwʾ—2p, 0d; *tbwʾ*—6p, 1d; *ybwʾ*—2p, 1d; *nbwʾ*—2p, 0d; *ybʾw*—0p, 2d;
Waw + imperfect: wʾbʾ—0p, 1d; *wybʾ*—0p, 32d; *wtbʾ(n)*—0p, 2d; *wnbʾ*—0p, 0d; *wtbʾw*—0p, 0d; *wybʾw*—0p, 17d.[8]

From these data it is apparent that the use of *waw* in Qal forms of the verb is not random, but rather that it clusters in the absolute infinitive in three out of the twelve attested forms of the construct infinitive, one out of the three attested forms of the imperative, and in four out of the five attested forms of the imperfect. It is completely absent in the four attested forms of *waw* plus the imperfect, which constitute 52, or more than 50% of the 96 individual cases of the verb in Genesis. Of the nine forms with *plene* spelling, four are also represented by defective spelling, suggesting that the *plene* spelling was, at least in those cases, a matter of scribal preference.

Both A. Murtonen (1973-74: 69, 72-74) and M. Cohen (1976: 367-68, 373-81, and the English summary, p. 489), who have observed this selective placement of *waw* in the biblical text, conclude that it was restricted to those positions where the major liturgical dialects of Hebrew during the Second Temple period, proto-Tiberian and Samaritan, tended to render the vowel *ō*, but that

---

[7]Murtonen 1953: 46, 51-53. His conclusions (51) are here presented *verbatim:*

"So, if we leave D out of account for the present, the fixation in writing of the other parts of the Pentateuch seems to have followed in the following order: 1) The Decalogue, 2) the stories of E of the period before Eisodus, 3) the laws of Numb. xv, 4) the stories of E of the Fathers, 5) (nearly contemporary to 4)) the story of Exodus etc. in J, 6) the Book of Covenant and Numb. xxviii-xxx, 7) a new edition of the J stories of Exodus etc. with Elohistic additions, 8) the Holiness Code and beginning about the same time under a longer period a new edition of the parts of Pentateuch already written down with incorporating of new material into it perhaps in the following order: the J stories of the period before Eisodus, the P stories of the Fathers and of Exodus etc. with additions, the E story of Jethro's visit, and the laws incorporated in P. The apparently greater age of the P additions to the stories of Exodus in comparison with the independent P stories of the same period may be due to the influence of the still older JE stories. 9) The final edition of the Pentateuch with addition of the J and P stories of the primaeval history, the additional stories in the second part of Numbers perhaps with incorporating of the laws Numb. xv, xxviii-xxx already written down and surely Numb. xix. 10) Later alterations of individual stories, e.g. Gen. v proved also by Samaritanus and LXX with its abundant use of vowel-consonants. It is probable that this order constructed exclusively on the ground of the use of the vowel-consonants does not hold good in every single detail, especially as regards shorter sections, but in the main features it seems to be valid, because in all the important points it agrees with the results of the most eminent representatives of the literary criticism arrived at from quite other premises and applying quite different methods."

W. L. Moran, in his review of *EHO* (1953: 365), criticized Murtonen's study by challenging its conclusions:

"It is striking that his methods lead him to date chapter 33 among the latest of the Deuteronomistic material [cf. Murtonen, p. 52], while Cross and Freedman date its writing in the 10th century!"

This challenge may be rebutted on two grounds: (1) Cross and Freedman (1975: 99, 105, n. 2) determined the date of Deut 33 by means of many criteria but certainly not by its orthography, since they restored the text to its purportedly original 10th-century orthography. (2) Murtonen (51-52) argues that the orthography, not the composition, is late; he explains that that orthography can only be used as an auxiliary method for establishing the date of composition.

[8]Cohen 1975: 61; cf. also Murtonen 1973-74: 70-74. For the orthography of the fem. pl. suffix *ōt*, cf. Cohen 1976: 374-81; Murtonen 1973-74: 75-81.

where they differed, the noncommital *defective* orthography was maintained.[9] Thus, the *plene* form *bbwʾ* was pronounced **b*^{e}*ḇō* in proto-Tiberian and **bābu* in Samaritan, while the defective *bʾ* was pronounced **bō* in the former and **ba* in the latter.[10]

Texts from the late post-Exilic period on demonstrate the proliferation of pre-Exilic and Exilic *m.l.* as well as some innovations, e.g., *waw* for *ā* and *ʾalep* for *ī* (Weinberg 1975: 463-64). These, however, fall beyond the chronological scope of this study.[11]

The implications of these conclusions for text-restoration are clear. From the 7th century on, Judean scribes had available to them a system of *matres lectionis* which they could use, if they wished, to indicate long vowels both in word final and medial positions. Judging from scribal practice as exemplified in the inscriptions and letters of this period, composition with *m.l.* was the norm rather than the exception. It can therefore be assumed that *m.l.* were employed in compositions originating during this period: Deuteronomy, the Deuteronomic history, Isaiah 1-39, Micah, Jeremiah, Habakkuk, etc.

A problem, however, arises with texts which were originally set down in writing in earlier centuries. This involves all of the texts dealt with by Cross and Freedman in *Ancient Yahwistic Poetry*, various documents and narratives now found in the Pentateuch, Joshua, Judges, 1 and 2 Samuel, 1 and 2 Kings, Amos, Hosea, as well as parts of Psalms (Hurvitz 1972; Robertson 1972; Polzin 1976). In these texts it may be assumed that in some cases, especially when the text was clear and unambiguous, scribes recopying them in the 7th-6th centuries may have done no more than add final *m.l.* However, in texts whose language was archaic or whose meaning was not obvious, these scribes may have gone further, adding medial *m.l.* as a rudimentary form of interpretation. It is therefore incumbent upon the contemporary scholar who suggests that the *m.l.* in a pre-7th-century text misrepresent the meaning of the original author to explain why a scribe in that period of the transmission of the text added the *m.l.*, especially if a final *m.l.* is involved.[12] These early additions cannot be ignored, because they date from a period in which the language of the texts set down in preceding centuries should still have been clear, at least to the members of those circles—the royal secretariat, temple scribes, and prophetic disciples—in which they were preserved and transmitted. There had not yet been a major catastrophe, such as the Exile, which involved the dislocation of the learned circles. To ignore these early *m.l.* is, in fact, to ignore linguistic traditions from the biblical period about the biblical text.

There does not appear to be any certain method of discerning whether or not *m.l.* characteristic of the 7th-6th centuries B.C.E. were in fact introduced into a given text during the post-Exilic period. Nevertheless, Murtonen's observation of the clustering of post-Exilic usages of *m.l.* in certain parts of the Pentateuch seems to provide a rule of thumb.

If in a given text there is a relatively high ratio of *plene* spellings—employing the *m.l.* which spread in certain forms during the post-Exilic period—to *defective* spellings in the same forms (cf. pp. 32-33),

[9]What role, if any, this socio-linguistic factor may have played in the emergence of an official text remains to be discussed. Cf. Talmon 1975: 325-26.

[10]Cf. Cohen 1976: 367-68. Cohen demonstrates, *contra* Purvis (1968: 52-69), that the same restricted secondary use of *waw* as a *m.l.* is characteristic of the Samaritan Pentateuch (= SP), whose orthography is not more *plene* than that of the MT (1975: 59-63). Murtonen, in fact (1973-74: 71-73), notes a tendency in medieval Samaritan manuscripts of the Pentateuch toward the elimination of some of these *m.l.* in places where the orthography of the SP = MT, but where it disagrees with the Samaritan reading traditions.

[11]Weinberg's study chronicles the different types of *plene* orthography but does not adequately treat the relationship between the orthography and the phonology of the language. His footnotes, however, are replete with references to studies where aspects of this relationship have been discussed. Cf. especially Kutscher 1974: 1-89.

[12]Thus, Cross and Freedman (1975: 99) restore Deut 33:2a *β ʾt-m rbbt qdš*<*m*> (for MT *wʾth mrbbt qdš*) and translate, "with him were myriads of holy ones. . . ." The MT orthography here apparently preserves the 7th-6th-century *m.l. he* (= *ō*), and the tradition of interpreting it "with him." (The MT vocalization reflects a different, possibly late, tradition of interpretation of the text, since the Targum translated this *wʿmh*, "and with him," and in the Samaritan tradition, the *he* was replaced by *waw* as a *m.l.* for *ō* [cf. pp. 105-6]).

it may be concluded that the orthography of that text was fixed late (Murtonen 1953: 49, 51). (The wholesale employment of *m.l.* in the sectarian scrolls from Qumrân indicates the direction in which the orthography of biblical texts might have developed had not early conventions fixed the writing of at least official texts.) Conversely, if *defective* spellings predominate, it may be concluded that the orthography was fixed early.[13] It stands to reason, then, that in texts of pre-Exilic origin whose orthography was fixed late, post-Exilic scribes may be responsible for *m.l.* of the type added in the pre-Exilic period. Where, however, the indications are that the orthography was fixed early, the likelihood is great that the *m.l.* originated in the activity of pre-Exilic scribes. Despite the apparent logic of this conclusion, a caveat is nevertheless necessary. The tentative nature of the results of such an undertaking in the present state of knowledge is obvious and an agnostic attitude toward them would be warranted.

[13]The quantitative factor introduced into these considerations is problematic. The orthographic profile developed by Murtonen (1953: 49-50), which determined the ratios of *defective* to *plene* orthography of the post-Exilic type in different parts of the Pentateuch, cannot be employed. Murtonen himself (1973-74: 66-68) has criticized his initial categorization of the post-Exilic, secondary usages of *waw* which formed the basis of his pioneering study. The conclusions in his second study, as well as those of M. Cohen in both of his articles (1975; 1976), indicate that many of the *defective* forms which were contrasted to *plene* ones must be eliminated from consideration since scribal convention precluded their ever being spelled *plene*. (Cf. above pp. 32-34.)

BIBLIOGRAPHY

Aharoni, M.

1975 Some Observations on the Recent Article by Y. Yadin in *BASOR* 222. *Bulletin of the American Schools of Oriental Research* 225: 67-68.

Aharoni, M., and Aharoni, Y.

1976 The Stratification of Judahite Sites in the 8th and 7th Centuries B.C.E. *Bulletin of the American Schools of Oriental Research* 224: 73-90.

Aharoni, Y.

1966a Hebrew Ostraca from Tel Arad. *Israel Exploration Journal* 16: 1-7.

1966b The Use of Hieratic Numerals in Hebrew Ostraca and the Shekel Weights. *Bulletin of the American Schools of Oriental Research* 184: 13-19.

1967a *The Land of the Bible: A Historical Geography.* Trans. A. F. Rainey from Hebrew, 1962, 1967. Philadelphia: Westminster.

1967b Seals of Royal Functionaries from Arad. *Eretz-Israel* 8: 101-3.

1967c The 'Persian Fortress' at Lachish—An Assyrian Palace? *Bulletin of the Israel Exploration Society* 31: 80-91.

1968 Trial Excavation in the 'Solar Shrine' at Lachish: Preliminary Report. *Israel Exploration Journal* 18: 157-69.

1969a The Israelite Sanctuary at Arad. Pp. 25-39 in *New Directions in Biblical Archeology*, eds. D. N. Freedman and J. C. Greenfield. Garden City, NY: Doubleday.

1969b Three Hebrew Ostraca from Arad. *Eretz-Israel* 9: 10-21.

1970 Three Hebrew Ostraca from Arad. *Bulletin of the American Schools of Oriental Research* 197: 16-41.

1973 *Beer-Sheba I.* Tel-Aviv: Tel-Aviv University/Institute of Archeology.

1975 *Arad Inscriptions.* Jerusalem: Bialik Institute Hebrew).

AI See Aharoni 1975.

Albright, W. F.

1943 The Gezer Calendar. *Bulletin of the American Schools of Oriental Research* 92: 16-26.

1944 The Oracles of Balaam. *Journal of Biblical Literature* 63: 207-33.

1966 *The Proto-Sinaitic Inscriptions and their Decipherment.* Cambridge, MA: Harvard University.

Amusin, J. D., and Heltzer, M. L.

1964 The Inscription from Meṣad Ḥashavyahu. *Israel Exploration Journal* 14: 148-57.

ANET See Pritchard 1955.

Avigad, N.

1945-46 The Inscription in the Bene Hezir Tomb. *Yediot* (= *Bulletin of the Jewish Palestine Exploration Society*) 12: 57-61.

1952 An Ammonite Seal. *Israel Exploration Journal* 2: 163-64.

1953 The Epitaph of a Royal Steward from Silwan Village. *Israel Exploration Journal* 3: 137-52.

1955 The Second Epitaph of a Royal Steward. *Israel Exploration Journal* 5: 163-67.

1961 The Jotham Seal from Elath. *Bulletin of the American Schools of Oriental Research* 163: 18-22.

1968 Notes on Some Inscribed Syro-Phoenician Seals. *Bulletin of the American Schools of Oriental Research* 189: 44-49.

1969 A Group of Hebrew Seals. *Eretz-Israel* 9: 1-9.

1970 Ammonite and Moabite Seals. Pp. 284-95 in *Near Eastern Archeology in the Twentieth Century: Essays in Honor of Nelson Glueck*, ed. J. A. Sanders. Garden City, NY: Doubleday.

1972 Two Inscriptions on Wine Jars. *Israel Exploration Journal* 22: 1-9.

1975 New Names on Hebrew Seals. *Eretz-Israel* 12: 66-71.

Bange, L. A.

1971 *A Study in the Use of Vowel-Letters in Alphabetic Consonantal Writing.* Munich: UNI-DRUCK.

Bar-Adon, P.

1975 An Early Hebrew Graffito in a Judean Cave. *Israel Exploration Journal* 25: 226-32.

Barr, J.

1968 *Comparative Philology and the Text of the Old Testament.* Oxford: Clarendon.

Barth, J.

1894 *Die Nominalbildung in den Semitischen Sprachen.* Hildesheim: Georg Olms, 1967. (Reproduced from the second edition, Leipzig, 1894.)

1906 Formangleichung bei begrifflichen Korrespondenzen. Pp. 787-96 in *Orientalische Studien . . . Th. Noeldeke*, ed. C. Bezold. Giesen: Alfred Topelmann.

1913 *Die Pronominalbildung in den Semitischen Sprachen.* Hildesheim: Georg Olms, 1967. (Reproduced from first edition, Leipzig, 1913.)

Bartlett, J. R.

1976 The Seal of ḤNH from the Neighborhood of Tell Ed-duweir. *Palestine Exploration Quarterly* 108: 59-61.

Bauer, H., and Leander, P.

1922 *Historische Grammatik der hebräischen Sprache.* Hildesheim: Georg Olms, 1962. (Reproduced from the first edition, Halle, 1922.)

Baumgartner, W.,

1954 Review of *Early Hebrew Orthography. Journal of Biblical Literature* 73: 259-61.

BDB See Brown, Driver, and Briggs 1906.

Beeston, A. F. L.

1962 *A Descriptive Grammar of Epigraphic South Arabian.* London: Luzac.

Ben-Hayyim, Z.

1954 *Studies in the Traditions of the Hebrew Language.* Madrid-Barcelona: Instituto "Arias Montano."

1978 Thoughts on the Hebrew Vowel System. Pp. 95-105 in *Studies in Bible and the Ancient Near East Presented to Samuel E. Loewenstamm* (Hebrew Volume), eds. Y. Avishur and J. Blau. Jerusalem: E. Rubinstein.

Bergstrasser, G.

1918 *Hebräische Grammatik I/II.* Hildesheim: Georg Olms, 1962. (First printed, Leipzig, 1918.)

Blau, J.

1966 Review of S. Moscati *et alia, An Introduction to the Comparative Grammar of the Semitic Languages*, 1964. *Lešonenu* 30: 136-56.

1968a Some Difficulties in the Reconstruction of 'Proto-Hebrew' and 'Proto-Canaanite.' *Beihefte zur Zeitschrift für die alttestamentliche Wissenschaft* 103 (= *In Memoriam Paul Kahle*): 29-43.

1968b ᶜẹśrẹ<*ᶜiśrayh (followed by a short vowel). *Lešonenu* 32: 267-68.

1970a Notes on Changes in Accent in Early Hebrew. Pp. 27-38 in *Hayyim Schirmann Jubilee Volume*, eds. S. Abramson and A. Mirsky. Jerusalem: Schocken Institute for Jewish Research.

1970b *On Pseudo-Corrections in Some Semitic Languages.* Jerusalem: Israel Academy of Sciences and Humanities.

1972 *Tōrat Hahege Wᵉhaṣṣūrōt.* Israel: Hakkibutz Hameuchad.

1976 *A Grammar of Biblical Hebrew.* Wiesbaden: Harrassowitz.

1977 "Weak" Phonetic Change and the Hebrew Śîn. *Hebrew Annual Review* 1: 67-119.

Blau, J., and Loewenstamm, S. E.

1970 Zur Frage der Scriptio Plena im Ugaritischen und Verwandtes. *Ugaritische Forschungen* 2: 19-33.

Bloomfield, L.

1933 *Language.* New York: Holt, Rinehart, and Winston.

Bordreuil, P.

1973 Inscriptions sigillaires ouest-sémitiques I: Epigraphie ammonite. *Syria* 50: 181-95.

1975 Inscriptions sigillaires ouest-sémitiques II: Un cachet récemment acquis par le Cabinet das médailles de la Bibliothèque Nationale. *Syria* 52: 107-18.

Bordreuil, P., and Lemaire, A.

1974 Trois Sceaux nord-ouest sémitiques inédits. *Semitica* 24: 25-34.

Bratsiotis, N. P.

1974 *ᵓyš ᵓîsh; ᵓšh ᵓishāh.* Pp. 225-35 in *Theological Dictionary of the Old Testament*, eds. G. J. Botterweck and H. Ringgren. Trans. J. T. Willis from German. Grand Rapids: Eerdmans. (Revised edition.)

Brockelmann, C.

1913 *Grundriss Der Vergleichenden Grammatik Der semitischen Sprachen, I, II.* Hildesheim: Georg Olms, 1966. (Originally published in two volumes, Berlin, 1908 and 1913.)

1956 *Hebräische Syntax.* Glückstadt: Neukirchen Kreis Moers.

Brown, F., Driver, S. R.; and Briggs, C. A.

1906 *Hebrew and English Lexicon of the Old Testament.* Oxford: Clarendon. (Reissued with corrections by G. R. Driver, 1951.)

Christensen, D. L.

1974 Num 21:14-15 and the Book of the Wars of Yahweh. *Catholic Biblical Quarterly* 36: 359-60.

Cody, A.

1970 A New Inscription from Tell al-Rimāḥ and King Jehoash of Israel. *Catholic Biblical Quarterly* 32: 325-40.

Cohen, M.

1975 The Orthography of the Samaritan Pentateuch. *Beth Mikra* 64: 54-70.

1976 The Orthography of the Samaritan Pentateuch, its Place in the History of Orthography and its Relation with the MT Orthography. *Beth Mikra* 66: 361-91.

Cross, F. M., and Freedman, D. N.

1952 *Early Hebrew Orthography: A Study of the Epigraphic Evidence.* American Oriental Series 36. New Haven: American Oriental Society.

1972 Some Observations on Early Hebrew. *Biblica* 53: 413-20.

1975 *Studies in Ancient Yahwistic Poetry.* A dissertation submitted to the Johns Hopkins University, Baltimore, MD, 1950. Society of Biblical Literature Dissertation Series 21. Missoula, MT: Scholars Press.

Cross, F. M., and Saley, R. J.

1970 Phoenician Inscriptions on a Plaque of the Seventh Century B.C. from Arslan Tash in Upper Syria. *Bulletin of the American Schools of Oriental Research* 197: 42-49.

Crowfoot, J. W.; Crowfoot, G. M.; and Kenyon, K. M.

1957 *The Objects from Samaria.* London: Palestine Exploration Fund.

Davidson, A. B.

1901 *Hebrew Syntax.* Edinburgh: T. & T. Clark.

Degen, R.

1969 *Altaramäische Grammatik der Inschriften des 10-8 Jh v. Chr.* Wiesbaden: Deutsche Morgenländische Gesellschaft.

Della Vida, G. Levi.

1968 The Shiloaḥ Inscription Reconsidered. *Beihefte zur Zeitschrift für die alttestamentliche Wissenschaft* 103: 162-66.

Demsky, A.
1977 A Proto-Canaanite Abecedary Dating from the Period of the Judges and Its Implications for the History of the Alphabet. *Tel-Aviv* 4: 14-27.

Dever, W. G.
1970 Iron Age Epigraphic Material from the Area of Khirbet El-Kom. *Hebrew Union College Annual* 40/41: 139-205.

Diem, W.
1974 Das Problem von *ś* im Althebräischen und die kanaanäische Lautvershiebung. *Zeitschrift der deutschen morgenländischen Gesellschaft* 124: 221-52.

Dietrich, M., and Loretz, O.
1967 Zur Ugaritische Lexicographie II. *Orientalische Literaturzeitung* 62: 533-51.

Dietrich, M.; Loretz, O.; and Sanmartín, J.
1974 Das reduzierte Keilalphabet. *Ugaritische Forschungen* 6: 15-18.
1975a Entzifferung und Transkription von RS 22.03. *Ugaritische Forschungen* 7: 548-49.
1975b Untersuchungen zur Schrift- und Lautlehre des Ugaritischen (IV): *w* als Mater lectionis in *bwtm* und *kwt*. *Ugaritische Forschungen* 7: 559-60.

Dahood, M.
1965-70 *Psalms I, II, III*. Garden City, NY: Doubleday.
1972 Review of D. W. Goodwin (1969). *Journal of the American Oriental Society* 92: 184-85.

Dion, P-E.
1974 *La Lange de Yaʾudi*. Canada: Corporation for the Publication of Academic Studies in Religion in Canada.

Diringer, D.
1934 *Le iscrizioni antico-ebraiche palestinesi*. Florence: Felice le Monnier.

DISO See Jean and Hoftijzer 1965.

Donner, H., and Röllig, W.
1964 *Kanaanäische und Aramäische Inschriften*. 3 volumes. Wiesbaden: Harrassowitz.

Dotan, A.
1971 Masorah. Cols. 1401-82 in *Encyclopaedia Judaica*, vol. 16. Jerusalem: Keter.

Driver, G. R.
1955 Hebrew Seals. *Palestine Exploration Quarterly* 87: 183.

EHO See Cross and Freedman 1952.

Eshel, B. Z.
1973 The Ending -ya(h) in Proper Names in Biblical Hebrew—is it Theophoric? Pp. 137-49 in *Proceedings of the Fifth World Congress of Jewish Studies*, vol. IV. Jerusalem: Hacohen. (English summary, pp. 273-74.)

Freedman, D. N.
1962 The Massoretic Text and the Qumran Scrolls: A Study in Orthography. *Textus* 2: 87-102.
1964 A Second Mesha Inscription. *Bulletin of the American Schools of Oriental Research* 175: 50-51.
1969 The Orthography of the Arad Ostraca. *Israel Exploration Journal* 19: 52-56.
1976 A Tour of the Tells. *American Schools of Oriental Research Newsletter*, no. 5 (Nov. 1976): 1-10 (complete issue).

Ganor, N. R.
1967 The Lachish Letters. *Palestine Exploration Quarterly* 99: 74-77.

Garbini, G.
1954-56 Note sul 'calendrio' di Gezer. *Annali dell'istituto orientale di Napoli* 6: 123-30.

Gevirtz, S.
1957 On the Etymology of the Phoenician Particle *ʾš*. *Journal of Near Eastern Studies* 16: 124-27.

Gibson, J. C. L.
1966 Stress and Vocalic Change in Hebrew: A Diachronic Study. *Journal of Linguistics* 2: 35-55.
1971 *Textbook of Syrian Semitic Inscriptions. Vol. I, Hebrew and Moabite Inscriptions*. Oxford: Clarendon.

Ginsburg, C. D.
1897 *Introduction to the Massoretico-Critical Edition of the Hebrew Bible* with a Prolegomenon by H. M. Orlinsky, "The Masoretic Text: A Critical Evaluation." New York: Ktav 1966. (Reprint of 1897 edition.)
1897-1905 *The Massorah Translated Into English With A Critical and Exegetical Commentary*, vol. IV. Vienna: Carl Fromme.

Ginsberg, H. L.
1935 Observations on the Lachish Documents. *Bulletin of the Jewish Palestine Exploration Society* 3: 77-86.
1938 Lachish Notes. *Bulletin of the American Schools of Oriental Research* 71: 24-25.
1942 Aramaic Studies Today. *Journal of the American Oriental Society* 62: 229-38.
1970 The Northwest Semitic Languages. Pp. 102-24 in *The World History of the Jewish People II, 1: Patriarchs*, ed. B. Mazar. Israel: Jewish History Publications.

GKC See Kautsch 1910.

Glueck, N.
1940 The Third Season of Excavation at Tell El-Kheleifeh. *Bulletin of the American Schools of Oriental Research* 79: 2-18.

Goetze, A.
1946 Number Idioms in Old Babylonian. *Journal of Near Eastern Studies* 5: 185-202.

Goodwin, D. W.
1969 *Text-Restoration Methods in Contemporary U. S. A. Biblical Scholarship*. Naples: Istituto Orientale Di Napoli.

Gordis, R.
1937 *The Biblical Text in the Making: A Study of the Kethib-Qere*. Philadelphia: The Dropsie College.

Gordon, C. H.
1965 *Ugaritic Textbook.* Analecta Orientalia 38. Rome: Biblical Institute.

Goshen-Gottstein, M.
1963 The Rise of the Tiberian Bible Text. Pp. 79-122 in *Biblical and Other Studies*, ed. A. Altman. Cambridge, MA: Harvard University.
1967 Hebrew Bible Manuscripts: Their History and Their Place in the *HUBP* Edition. *Biblica* 48: 243-90.

Grabbe, L. L.
1977 *Comparative Philology and the Text of Job: A Study in Methodology.* The Society of Biblical Literature Dissertation Series 34. Missoula, MT: Scholars Press.

Greenstein, E. L.
1976 A Phoenician Inscription in Ugaritic Script? *Journal of the Ancient Near Eastern Society* 8: 49-57.

Harris, Z. S.
1936 *A Grammar of the Phoenician Language.* American Oriental Society Series 8. New Haven: American Oriental Society.
1939 *Development of the Canaanite Dialects.* American Oriental Series 16. New Haven: American Oriental Society.

Herr, L. G.
1978 *The Scripts of Ancient Northwest Semitic Seals.* Harvard Semitic Monographs 18. Missoula, MT: Scholars Press.

Herzog, Z.; Rainey, A. F.; and Moshkovitz, Sh.
1977 The Stratigraphy at Beer-Sheba and the Location of the Sanctuary. *Bulletin of the American Schools of Oriental Research* 225: 49-58.

Hoftijzer, J.
1963 La Nota Accusativi *ʾt* en Phénicien. *Le Museon* 76: 195-200.

Horn, S. H.
1969 The Amman Citadel Inscription. *Bulletin of the American Schools of Oriental Research* 193: 2-13.

Hurvitz, A.
1972 *The Transition Period in Biblical Hebrew: A Study in Post-Exilic Hebrew and its Implications for Dating of Psalms.* Jerusalem: Bialik Insitiute.

Japhet, S.
1968 The Supposed Common Authorship of Chronicles and Ezra-Nehemia Investigated Anew. *Vetus Testamentum* 18: 330-71.

Jean, C. F., and Hoftijzer, J.
1965 *Dictionnaire des inscriptions sémitiques de l'ouest.* Leiden: Brill.

Joüon, P. P.
1923 *Grammaire de l'hébreu biblique.* Rome: Biblical Institute.

Kahle, P.
1960 *The Cairo Geniza,* 2nd edition. London: Praeger.

KAI See Donner and Röllig 1962-64.

Kautsch, E.
1910 *Genesius' Hebrew Grammar*, ed. E. Kautsch, trans. A. E. Cowley. Oxford: Clarendon.

KB See Koehler and Baumgartner 1953.

Kochavi, M.
1977 An Ostracon of the Period of the Judges from ᶜIzbet Ṣarṭah. *Tel-Aviv* 4: 1-13.

Koehler, L., and Baumgartner, W.
1953 *Lexicon in Veteris Testamenti Libros.* Leiden: Brill.

Koopmans, J. J.
1962 *Aramäische Chrestomathie I.* Leiden: Nederlands Instituut Voor Het Nabije Oosten.

Kutscher, E. Y.
1967 Additional Remarks About Gordon's Book. *Lešonenu* 31: 33-36.
1968 Reply to Prof. Loewenstamm. *Lešonenu* 32: 374-75.
1971 Hebrew Language: The Dead Sea Scrolls, Mishnaic. Cols. 1583-1607 in *Encyclopaedia Judaica,* vol. 16. Jerusalem: Keter.
1972 *A History of Aramaic, Part I.* Jerusalem: Akademon (Hebrew).
1974 *The Language and Linguistic Background of the Isaiah Scroll (IQIsa*[a]*).* Leiden: Brill. (Hebrew original, 1969.)
1976 *Studies in Galilean Aramaic.* Trans. M. Sokoloff from Hebrew, 1950-52. Ramat Gan: Bar Ilan University.

Lance, H. D.
1971 The Royal Stamps and the Kingdom of Josiah. *Harvard Theological Review* 64: 315-32.

Lane, W. R.
1961 Newly Recognized Occurrences of the Weight-Name PYM. *Bulletin of the American Schools of Oriental Research* 164: 21-23.

Lemaire, A.
1975a Remarques sur la datation des estamplilles, lmlk. *Vetus Testamentum* 25: 678-82.
1975b *Zamīr* dans la tablette de Gezer et le Cantique des Cantiques. *Vetus Testamentum* 25: 15-26.
1976 Prieres en temps de crise: les inscriptions de Khirbet Beit Lei. *Revue biblique* 83: 558-68.
1977a *Inscriptions hébräiques, tome I: Les ostraca.* Paris: Editions du Cerf.
1977b Les inscriptions de Khirbet El-Qôm et l'Ashérah de YHWH. *Revue biblique* 84: 595-608.

Loewenstamm, S. E.
1968 *Matres Lectionis* in Ugaritic. *Lešonenu* 32: 369-73.
1969 Yod as a *Mater Lectionis* in Ugaritic. *Lešonenu* 33: 111-14.

Maisler, B.
1950 Two Hebrew Ostraca from Tell Qasile. *Journal of Near Eastern Studies* 10: 265-67.

Malamat, A.
1971 On the Akkadian Transcription of the Name of King Joash. *Bulletin of the American Schools of Oriental Research* 204: 37-40.

Malmberg, B.
1963 *Phonetics*. New York: Dover.

McCarter, P. K.
1974 "Yaw, Son of Omri": A Philological Note on Israelite Chronology. *Bulletin of the American Schools of Oriental Research* 216: 5-7.
1975 *The Antiquity of the Greek Alphabet and the Early Phoenician Scripts*. Harvard Semitic Monograph 9. Missoula, MT: Scholars Press.

Mendenhall, G. E.
1971 A New Chapter in the History of the Alphabet. *Bulletin du Musée le Beyrouth* 24: 13-18.
1978 On the History of Writing. *Biblical Archeologist* 41: 134-35.

Meshel, Z.
1975 On the Problem of Tell el-Kheleifeh, Elath, and Ezion-Geber. *Eretz-Israel* 12: 49-56.
1978 *Kuntillet ᶜAjrud: A Religious Centre from the Time of the Judaean Monarchy on the Border of Sinai.* Israel Museum Cat. No. 175.

Meshel, Z., and Meyers, C.
1976 The Name of God in the Wilderness of Zin. *Biblical Archeologist* 39: 6-10.

Miller, E. F.
1927 *The Influence of Gesenius on Hebrew Lexicography*. New York: AMS Press, 1966. (Reprint of the 1927 edition.)

Morag, S.
1958 *Mēšaᶜ*: A Study of Certain Features of Old Hebrew Dialects. *Eretz-Israel* 5: 138-44.
1962 *The Vocalization Systems of Arabic, Hebrew, and Aramaic.* = Janua Linguarum 13. The Hague: Mouton.

Moran, W.
1953 Review of *Early Hebrew Orthography*. *Catholic Biblical Quarterly* 15: 364-67.
1965 The Hebrew Language against its Northwest Semitic Background. Pp. 59-84 in *The Bible and the Ancient Near East: Essays . . . W. F. Albright*, ed. G. E. Wright. Garden City, NY: Doubleday.

Moscati, S.
1951 *L'epigrafia ebraica antica*. Rome: Biblical Institute.
1954 Review of *Early Hebrew Orthography*. *Journal of Near Eastern Studies* 13: 133-35.

Moscati, S., et al.
1964 *An Introduction to the Comparative Grammar of the Semitic Languages*. Weisbaden: Harrassowitz.

Murtonen, A.
1953 The Fixation in Writing of Various Parts of the Pentateuch. *Vetus Testamentum* 3: 46-53.
1973-74 On the Interpretation of the *Matres Lectionis* in Biblical Hebrew. *Abr-Nahrain* 14: 66-121.

Naveh, J.
1960 A Hebrew Letter from the Seventh Century. *Israel Exploration Journal* 10: 129-39.
1963 Old Hebrew Inscriptions in a Burial Cave. *Israel Exploration Journal* 13: 74-92.
1968 A Palaeographic Note on the Distribution of the Hebrew Script. *Harvard Theological Revue* 61: 68-74.
1970a The Scripts in Palestine and Transjordan in the Iron Age. Pp. 277-83 in *Near Eastern Archeology in the Twentieth Century: Essays in Honor of Nelson Glueck*, ed. J. A. Sanders. Garden City, NY: Doubleday.
1970b *The Development of the Aramaic Script*. Jerusalem: Israel Academy of Sciences and Humanities.
1978 Some Observations on the Ostracon from ᶜIzbet Ṣarṭah. *Israel Exploration Journal* 28: 31-35.

Noeldeke, Th.
1910 *Neue Beiträge zur Semitischen Sprachwissenschaft.* Strassburg: Karl J. Trübner.

Norin, S.
1979 Jô-Namen und Jᵉhô-Namen. *Vetus Testamentum* 39: 87-97.

Noth, M.
1928 *Die Israelitischen Personennamen im Rahmen der Gemeinsemitischen Namengebung*. Stuttgart: Kohlhammer.

Nylander, C.
1967 A Note on the Stonecutting and Masonry of Tel Arad. *Israel Exploration Journal* 17: 56-59.

Orlinsky, H. M.
1966 The Masoretic Text: A Critical Evaluation. Prolegomenon to KTAV Reprint of Ginsburg, C. D. *Introduction to the Massoretico-Critical Edition of the Hebrew Bible*, 1897. New York: Ktav. Pp I-XXXVII.

Pardee, D.
1978 The Judicial Plea from Meṣad Ḥashavyahu (Yavneh Yam): A New Philological Study. *Maarav* 1: 33-66.

Parunak, H. V. D.
1978 The Orthography of the Arad Ostraca. *Bulletin of the American Schools of Oriental Research* 230: 25-31.

Polzin, R.
1976 *Late Biblical Hebrew: Toward an Historical Typology of Biblical Hebrew Prose.* Harvard Semitic Monographs 12. Missoula, MT: Scholars Press.

Porten, B.
1971 The Aramaic Marriage Contract of the Handmaiden Tamut (Hebrew). Pp. 307-29 in *Bible and Jewish History, Studies . . . Dedicated to the Memory of Jacob Liver*, ed. B. Uffenheimer. Tel-Aviv: Tel-Aviv University.

Pritchard, J. B.
1955 *Ancient Near Eastern Texts Relating to the Old Testament*², ed. J. B. Pritchard. Princeton: Princeton University.

1969 *The Ancient Near East: Supplementary Texts and Pictures Relating to the Old Testament*, ed. J. B. Pritchard. Princeton: Princeton University.

Purvis, J. D.
1968 *The Samaritan Pentateuch and the Origin of the Samaritan Sect.* Harvard Semitic Monographs 2. Cambridge: Harvard University.

Qimron, E.
1976 *A Grammar of the Hebrew Language of the Dead Sea Scrolls.* Ph.D. thesis submitted to the Senate of the Hebrew University.

Rabin, C.
1971 *ʿibrīt.* Cols. 51-73 in *Encyclopaedia Biblica*, vol. 6. Jerusalem: Bialik Institute.

Rainey, A. F.
1970 Semantic Parallels to the Samaria Ostraca. *Palestine Exploration Quarterly* 102: 42-51.
1972 The Word *Ywm* in Ugaritic and in Hebrew. *Lešonenu* 36: 186-89.
1977 Three Additional Ostraca from Arad. *Tel-Aviv* 4: 97-102.

Richardson, H. N.
1971 The Last Words of David: Some Notes on II Samuel 23:1-7. *Journal of Biblical Literature* 110: 257-66.

Robertson, David A.
1972 *Linguistic Evidence in Dating Early Hebrew Poetry.* The Society of Biblical Literature Dissertation Series 3. Missoula, MT: Scholars Press.

Rocco, B.
1970 Alla Ricerca di un'etimologia (mʾš/mš). *Annali dell'istituto orientale di Napoli* 30: 396-99.

Rosenthal, F.
1953 Review of *Early Hebrew Orthography. Journal of the American Oriental Society* 73: 46-47.
1976 Review of P.-E. Dion, *La langue de Yaʾudi*, 1974. *Journal of Biblical Literature* 95: 153-55.

Segert, S.
1961 Semitische Marginalien III, Zur Entstehung des aramäischen Artikels und der Mater Lectionis. *Archiv Orientali* 29: 117-18.

Shea, W. H.
1977 The Date and Significance of the Samaritan Ostraca. *Israel Exploration Journal* 27: 16-27.

Sherman, M. E.
1966 *Systems of Hebrew and Aramaic Orthography: An Epigraphic History of the Use of Matres Lectionis in Non-Biblical Texts to ca.* A.D. *135.* An unpublished dissertation submitted to Harvard Divinity School.

Speiser, E. A.
1940 Of Shoes and Shekels. *Bulletin of the American Schools of Oriental Research* 77: 15-20.

Sperber, A.
1939 Hebrew Based Upon Biblical Passages in Parallel Transmission. *Hebrew Union College Annual:* 153-249.
1943 *Hebrew Grammar: A New Approach.* New York: Jewish Theological Seminary.

Stern, E.
1962 Weights and Measures. Cols. 846-878 in *Encyclopaedia Biblica*, vol. 4. Jerusalem: Bialik Institute.

Stuart, D. K.
1976 *Studies in Early Hebrew Meter.* Harvard Semitic Monographs 13. Missoula, MT: Scholars Press.

Talmon, S.
1975 The Textual Study of the Bible—A New Outlook. Pp. 321-400 in *Qumran and the History of the Biblical Text*, eds. F. M. Cross and S. Talmon. Cambridge, MA: Harvard University.

Torczyner, N. H.
1938 *Lachish I: The Lachish Letters.* London: Oxford University.
1939 *Tʿwdwt Lkyš.* Jerusalem: Israel Exploration Society.

Tsevat, M.
1960 A Chapter on Old West Semitic Orthography. Pp. 89-91 in *The Joshua Bloch Memorial Volume: Studies in Booklore and History*, eds. A. Berger et al. New York: The New York Public Library.

Tushingham, A. D.
1971 A Royal Israelite Seal (?) and the Royal Jar Handle Stamps (Part Two). *Bulletin of the American Schools of Oriental Research* 201: 23-35.

Tzori, N.
1961 A Hebrew Ostracon from Beth Shean. *Yediot* 25: 145-46.

Ussishkin, D.
1976 Royal Judean Storage Jars and Private Seal Impressions. *Bulletin of the American Schools of Oriental Research* 223: 1-13.
1977 The Destruction of Lachish and the Dating of the Royal Judean Storage Jars. *Tel-Aviv* 4: 28-60.
1978 Excavations at Tel Lachish—1973-77, Preliminary Report. *Tel-Aviv* 5: 1-97.

UT See Gordon 1965.

Vattioni, F.
1969 I sigilli ebraici. *Biblica* 50: 357-88.

von Soden, W.
1969 *Grundriss der Akkadischen Grammatik.* Analecta Orientalia 33. Rome: Biblical Institute.

Weinberg, W.
1975 The History of Hebrew *Plene* Spelling: From Antiquity to Haskalah. *Hebrew Union College Annual* 46: 457-87.

West, W. W.
1978 Review of P. K. McCarter 1975. *Journal of the American Oriental Society* 98: 346-47.

Wevers, J. W.
1970 *Ḥeth* in Classical Hebrew. Pp. 101-12 in *Essays on the Ancient Semitic World*, eds. J. W. Wevers and D. B. Redford. Canada: University of Toronto.

Windfuhr, G.
1970 The Cuneiform Signs of Ugarit. *Journal of Near Eastern Studies* 29: 48-51.

Yadin, Y.
1965 A Note on the Stratigraphy of Arad. *Israel Exploration Journal* 15: 180.

1976 Beer-Sheba: The High Place Destroyed by King Josiah. *Bulletin of the American Schools of Oriental Research* 222: 5-17.

Yalon, H.
1967 *Studies in The Dead Sea Scrolls (1949-1952).* Jerusalem: Kiryath Sefer.

Yeivin, S.
1962 The Judicial Petition from Meẕad Ḫashavyahu. *Bibliotheca Orientalis* 19: 3-10.

Zevit, Z.
1977 The Linguistic and Contextual Arguments in Favor of a Hebrew 3m.s. Suffix -Y. *Ugarit Forschungen* 9: 315-28.